I

Personal Year Vibrations

This book is dedicated to you, may it help you
on your journey through life.

"For everything there is a season
and a time for every matter under heaven."

—Ecclesiastes 3:1

## ACKNOWLEDGEMENTS – THANKS!

There are people who believed in my dream of writing this book, who encouraged me along the way, and to whom I'd like to give a special thanks: Larry Durbin, Judene Deakle, David Carter, Paul Pieper, Donna Dawdy, and Stacey Williams. Thanks to Ron Corveau for reminding me that this is what I'm supposed to do. Thanks to my children, Matt and Alicia, for their support and encouragement. A huge thanks to Racheal Lomas for designing the cover and bringing the book to fruition. Without her this book would still be sitting in a storage bin somewhere in my garage. And thanks to all of the people who allowed me to dissect their names throughout the years.

# CONTENTS

# AUTHOR'S NOTE

"You need to study numerology," my friend Debby said to me as she gathered up the playing cards from the table. She had just finished shocking me by laying out a deck of playing cards and predicting my future. The reading didn't shock me as much as the person who read them. Debby had been my friend for the past six months and I had no inkling that she had such a talent. Had I known, I'm sure I would have bugged her constantly to read my cards. Maybe that's why she never said anything about it before this evening.

"Numerology? That sounds like math," I said, "I suck at math."

"Whatever," she replied, "You just need to do it."

And so, for the past 31 years, I did.

I learned that numerology isn't math, but that you do need to know how to add numbers together. Numerology is an ancient science, studied in secrecy by Pythagoras around 500 BC. I learned what the numbers mean, studied and researched their symbolism, and paid attention to what's going on during different number vibrations. I spent many days and nights reading about and practicing numerology on anyone who would give me their birth date or birth certificate information. I analyzed hundreds of people. Everywhere I went I carried a pen and paper with me, always ready to amaze people (and myself) with numerology's accuracy.

Using numbers, I enjoy helping people to try to understand their circumstances and themselves a bit better. It's fun to meet complete strangers and tell them about their current situation just by knowing a few of their numbers. People are surprised by how much I am able to tell them about themselves by knowing the vibrations of the day they were born.

I noticed that there are no numerology books dedicated to the in-depth study of personal year cycles. In my opinion, these cycles are extremely important to know and understand because they are right here, right now, in-your-face vibrations. We live through them daily. Wouldn't life flow a little easier if we knew what the vibrations surrounding us were at specific times in our lives? Being prepared is good, knowledge is power.

In 1989, I started working on a numerology book about the personal year cycles. Since there are plenty of numerology websites on the Internet and numerology

## AUTHOR'S NOTE

books on the market that discuss life lessons, personality traits, abilities, and the history of numerology, I decided I wasn't about to reinvent the wheel and I have left that information out of this book.

It's best if you don't place a judgment on the years, good or bad, numbers are numbers. Some years may be more demanding than others, but if you're prepared ahead of time, you can be ready to handle any situation. Learn to understand what your personal year is trying to teach you and reflect on how much you grow.

Remember: *Attitude is the key.*

# INTRODUCTION

What's the best direction to take this year? Is this the month to take a vacation or stay home? Is this a day to socialize or to keep your nose to the grindstone? Is this a time to be aggressive or to sit back and cooperate?

When faced with a decision, when you want to know the probability of certain events, or when you just want some advice, this book can help. Personal Year Vibrations is a numerology book that describes the vibrations of each year, month, and day in detail, explaining exactly what you have to accomplish during the course of each year, and the attitudes needed in order to succeed. By going with the flow of each year you'll find you can accomplish everything you need to do. Knowing this, you can eliminate a lot of worry and speculation about what you think you ought to be doing.

Personal Year Vibrations describes the types of experiences you can expect to encounter and gives specific advice regarding the positive attitudes needed in order to produce beneficial results for growth, development, and success. As you read the descriptions, pay particular attention to the advice given and warnings of the consequences of unproductive behavior. Many personal problems can be solved by wisely following the instructions.

Help romance by looking up your love's year, month, or day. You might be able to figure out what kind of mood he or she is in, or why he or she is acting a certain way. I have thwarted many an argument with a boss, coworker, child, or lover, by simply figuring out what kind of day that person is having and learned not to take their words or actions to heart.

With the help of Personal Year Vibrations you can see why events scheduled on certain days are delayed, which month is better for business, or why some years produce the unexpected. By using the advice given, many mistakes can be avoided and opportunities can be taken advantage of at the right time.

Your personal years repeat in nine year cycles; each year in the nine year cycle has its own purpose. If the challenges of the cycle are faced and overcome, new opportunities are allowed to enter. Fighting, ignoring, or overreacting to circumstances will only cause the same or similar situations to reoccur.

## INTRODUCTION

**Personal Year 1:** Is a time to begin.

**Personal Year 2:** Is a time of cooperation.

**Personal Year 3:** Is a year for fun and creativity.

**Personal Year 4:** Is a year to keep your nose to the grindstone and to work hard.

**Personal Year 5:** Is full of opportunity, the catch is to remain constructive.

**Personal Year 6:** Is a time for love, responsibility, and balance.

**Personal Year 7:** Is a slow, introspective year.

**Personal Year 8:** Is one for business and dealing with finances.

**Personal Year 9:** Is a year of endings, to let go so you can begin again the following year.

Knowing where you are in the cycle of life, can help you determine, in advance, the times of greatest opportunity, or foresee problems and areas in which problems are likely to occur. You can also look back and understand why some past experiences were so pleasant while others felt so uncomfortable. It's quite interesting to look back at the different years and see what transpired.

Although many people may be looking for predictions of things to come, this is not a fortune-telling book. It cannot predict the actions you are going to take now or in the future. It can only predict the vibrations available to you at certain times in your life. What you do with the information is strictly up to you. Knowledge is power. Learn how to go with the tide, with the flow of life.

Personal Year Vibrations can be used throughout your entire lifetime, this book will not become obsolete. The information provided has been tested since 1988. I continue to be impressed by numerology's consistent accuracy. I can't tell you why numerology predictions are so accurate, only that they are. I have no doubt you will be pleasantly surprised by the detailed information and advice this book offers.

Ultimately, you must remember: Your life depends on what you choose to do in the circumstances in which you find yourself. Personal Year Vibrations accurately predicts the vibrations and cycles surrounding you, but it's up to you to act on the opportunities to create your own possibilities, achievements, and successes.

# HOW TO USE PERSONAL YEAR VIBRATIONS

Find your personal year number quickly and easily. It is the sum of the birth month, birth day, and the number of the year in question. For example, if your birthday is February 1 and you want to know what personal year you're in during 2011, calculate the following:

**Month + Day + Year**
February 1, 2011 =
2 + 1 + 4 (2011 reduced) = 7 personal year

If the birth month or day is made up of two digits (10, 11, or 12, etc). reduce the number to a single digit (1, 2, or 3, etc). and then continue adding. The sum is also reduced to a single digit. For example, if your birthday is October 12 and you want to know what personal year you're in during 2015, calculate the following:

**October 12, 2015 =**
1 (10 reduced) + 3 (12 reduced) + 8 (2015 reduced) = 3 (12 reduced)

To find the number of the year for any year in question, add the digits of the year together and reduce these to a single digit. See examples below:

**2019** = 2 + 0 + 1 + 9 = 12 = 1 + 2 = 3
**2011** = 2 + 0 + 1 + 1 = 4
**1986** = 1 + 9 + 8 + 6 = 24 = 2 + 4 = 6

Personal year cycles begin January 1st and end December 31st, they follow the calendar years. Read the description for your personal year to see what will be in store for you during the year. Then read the personal month descriptions, detailed after each personal year. They provide specific information with regard to feelings, experiences, and the attitudes to have in order to get ahead during the month. They also suggest ways to deal with situations in a more constructive manner. Some months are more active than others, and reading the advice given by the personal month can prove to be extremely beneficial.

To be prepared for the day, read the personal day description, which breaks down what each day has in store for you. Personal days describe the type of day you can expect to have, things for you to try to accomplish or to leave for another day, the negative tendencies to avoid and the positive attitudes for success. Refer to the personal day charts beginning on page 126.

It is also interesting to look back at past years, to read about the vibrations that were surrounding you at different times in your life. If you look back nine years, you'll find that this year you'll experience similar situations, challenges, and opportunities. That's because nine years ago the vibrations surrounding you were the same as they are now. Although your environment and circumstances may be different, you'll find that the underlying theme of the year is the same.

There are no bad numbers. It's your attitude about the situation you're in that creates a judgment. Going with the flow of the year will make life a little easier—you'll be swimming with the current instead of against it. It's your decision.

# 1 PERSONAL YEAR VIBRATION

You are about to embark on the start of an entirely new phase of your life. This is a year of dramatic change, progress, and new beginnings. This year's vibrations bring events and opportunities for you to move in a new direction which will ultimately improve your life.

You'll be faced with an important decision and will experience significant changes in your living conditions. You will likely change some aspects of your job or your residence. The change will probably be due to your own efforts and will trigger a sequence of events which in turn will produce substantial changes in almost every phase of your life. Follow your impulses, listen to your gut reactions, begin to visualize what you want most. Life is pushing you to move in a positive direction.

Your actions this year will have a significant effect on the course of the next nine years. In other words, if you delay or don't accept the changes offered this year or ignore the chance to expand, you may miss opportunities that depend on the changes, taking the steam out of the whole phase of the next nine years.

Don't allow fear to stand in your way. Don't let others talk you out of doing what you feel is best for you. Life is presenting you a chance to get out of your rut. If the odds are encouraging, forge ahead with new paths, plans, areas, and methods. If you develop a nonchalant attitude or listless habit during the year, it will be very difficult to break and you may end up getting stuck, back in your rut. Life is presenting this opportunity because you are ready for it. Grab it and move forward.

You must have courage, make plans, and avoid indecision. For the sake of progress and happiness, look to the future and be willing to change, advance, and prosper. Be determined. It may be necessary for you to let go of things having to do with the past so you can take advantage of new opportunities. There are still some things left over from last year that have you feeling somewhat uneasy or emotional. These relationships or activities will phase out of your life by August.

As terminations come, remind yourself that it's time for you to let go of relationships, liabilities, and habits that are nonproductive and are no longer a part of your future. Remember, this is a "beginning" time. Don't drift or have fear of the future, because if you do, you may lose out and miss the opportunity which is present. The opportunity is there, but it's up to you to seize it. Anything new that's begun this year is almost guaranteed to be successful, so don't be afraid of taking that seemingly gigantic and brave first step into the unknown.

Projects begun now will blossom in two years. Patience and perseverance are of utmost importance. Unions and partnerships you begin now will grow, although you'll find that relationships will be important and more comfortable to deal with next year. Even so, you'll experience extraordinary events in your love life. This is a year of sudden, impulsive love affairs which will be startling and somewhat disruptive.

You may have to make compromises to maintain present relationships; however, this is not the year to sacrifice yourself for others. It's time for you to make a clean break from dead or dying relationships which are a constant drain on your emotional energy. The people intended to remain with you for the next nine years will move along with this year's changes. Welcome new associates, both in business and in your social circle, as they have the potential to become lasting friends.

This year will not be easy and you will need to use a substantial amount of system and organization to get the results you want. You'll be forced to stand up for yourself, face any and all difficulties, and confront challenges head on. This year calls for conviction of purpose and clear thinking.

Life will test your courage, character, and willpower. In turn, you must show what you have and what you can do. It will be important for you to keep going, even when times seem difficult, for hidden opportunities abound if you are alert enough to recognize them.

Recognizing and acting on opportunities when they present themselves will produce rewards greater than you could imagine. Broaden your activities and meet conditions or circumstances which come up unexpectedly with executive ability and originality of thought. This is a time of struggle, but also a time of great reward. Follow your gut instincts, they will lead you in the right direction.

This is a year to convert ideas, aspirations, and dreams to reality. This year's vibration opens new opportunities in the job or business world. Promotions will be yours if you are determined and take the initiative. If you see no future in your present employment, investigate the market for other possibilities. Don't be afraid to try something that you have always wanted to do. Turn an avocation or hobby into a business. It's time for you to look for new ideas and new ways to get ahead.

Opportunities for advancement must be searched, researched, and investigated. They will not automatically fall into your lap. Study your goals, surroundings, and opportunities carefully and do not become impulsive or headstrong in making decisions regarding changes or in moving forward. It's important that you research the details and contemplate the possible consequences of your actions. Choose worthwhile projects that really excite you. Don't be afraid to take a chance with a new idea or plan. You may find more than one opportunity to exercise your ability to make decisions.

Mistakes will be inevitable. Realize that sometimes making mistakes is a means of gaining valuable knowledge and experience. If you learn from them, they're not really mistakes as long as you don't repeat them. Don't allow guilt or blame to enter your thoughts. You are entering unfamiliar territory and you can't be expected to know everything right off the bat. By the end of the year you will feel more confident in yourself and your abilities.

It will be necessary for you to be very open and honest, even blunt. Think of your own desires, though at times you may have to compromise. Friends and family members will most likely be surprised by the changes you make through your own efforts; be prepared for changes in family relationships. Your independent attitude may alienate those who love you, bringing unnecessary arguments, bickering, confrontations, and many emotional ups and downs. Make an extra effort to maintain peace. Try to keep in mind that family members love you and want what they feel is best for you. Let them know that you understand their fears, but ultimately you will have to do what you have to do. This is your life, not theirs.

Emphasize your independence. Travel and see the world. If there are areas where you have been dependent, this is a time to work on them. Give up bad habits which you have fallen into over the past nine years. Quit smoking. Quit drinking to excess. Give up drugs and gambling. If existing conditions have been bothering you for some time, this is the time to start to break-free. Develop more self-confidence, learn how to be assertive and express yourself with courage. Don't be a "yes" man or woman any longer. Say something if you feel that things are not quite right, don't just sit back and suffer.

If you are prepared to make the effort, this will be an excellent year for personal development and expressing your individuality. By the end of the year you will feel greater self-respect, have more knowledge, and increase your ability to stand on your own two feet. It's time for you to have a receptive attitude and look forward to the coming nine-year cycle with hope, faith, optimism, and enthusiasm.

# 1 PERSONAL YEAR VIBRATION

## Personal Month Vibrations (1 PY)

The following is a brief outline of the vibrations you can expect during the 1 Personal Year (for a more detailed description of what a specific month has in store for you, read the information found under the month heading, at the end of this section).

This year, it's up to you to do the thinking and planning for yourself. You may not fully understand this until fall, even though several times during the spring and summer you will be required to make vital decisions concerning your future and what you want out of life. During the spring and summer take care of your health and that of loved ones. Make the effort to be more constructive; avoid shortcuts and irresponsible behavior. Between January and August you will have the opportunity to tie up loose ends that have been left hanging from the preceding year.

January through March, build relationships and establish a new foundation. Although you feel the urge to act, this is not the time to be ambitious or to make any material changes. Allow yourself to end relationships or activities satisfactorily. Situations will arise requiring you to have an attractive appearance and to put on a happy face.

In February you may move, travel or take a short vacation. A relationship or activity ready for completion may require an imaginative approach to bring it to an end.

During March changes may be made in business, work, career, or in your family situation. Reconstruct plans or projects and take care of any mistakes in finance or judgment. You must put everything in order to get new ventures underway. Research ideas and don't gamble on the unknown. Work instead of talking about what needs to be done.

During the spring you'll start to feel the vibrations of the year beginning to come through. Sometime in April there will be a break as chances for expansion and opportunity present themselves. Start to act now for improvement. Take a chance on luck and love, although love affairs may not last. Watch legal commitments and expect conflicts and outbursts.

May will likely be an emotional time with demands from work, friends and home. Rest, have poise and say very little. Serving others may open doors to new opportunities. Try not to be stubborn.

Use June to implement new goals and release fixed habits and attitudes which no longer are productive. You may experience some loneliness or a lack of social life. Spend time in the country or change your diet and exercise. Take care of your health.

July offers a chance for you to take control, to plan, build and act. You may have to make a major decision involving money. Use good judgment, and think of the consequences.

August and September may bring things to a head. The projects, activities, or relationships that began last October are either completed or abandoned to help you move forward into the next nine years.

In September you may be off to a new start or beginning that could prove to be temporary. Others may challenge some of your ideas. Use originality and creativity, but don't go overboard and irritate or alienate others. You may experience altercations in your personal relationships. Autumn will open the way to new opportunities and decisions you may not have counted upon.

During October you may experience setbacks involving other people's schedules, unfinished details, illness, or a lack of money. Although the year has been full of false starts and wrong turns, keep moving forward as you may be able to work out your plans earlier than anticipated.

November is an excellent time for a sales promotion and involving others in your new ventures. You may experience a brief separation from your mate. Try to keep your emotions in balance.

In December, be very wise and get down to work in a concrete and practical manner, upon your former plans. Let things fall into place without forcing or persuading the issues. You may find you have too little money unless you saved all year. Hard work now will pay off later.

Remember during a 1 Personal Year Vibration: Start something, develop new ideas, seek out new opportunities, express your individuality, act with self-confidence and the courage of your convictions.

## January Vibrations (1 PY)

This month offers an opportunity for you to interact with friends and lovers and to make others happy. Socializing with old friends and longtime acquaintances could put you in contact with new and special people. Attending unusual social gatherings might bring in the contacts who will assist you at a future time.

Although you feel the urge to act, this isn't the time to be ambitious or to make any material changes. Instead, this is a time for you to work quietly, to take care of the details that may slow you down later. Pushing your own work to the forefront isn't advisable this month, as the time for ambition is coming later during the year. Wait patiently for developments, even though it may seem as though nothing is happening.

Rest and allow friends, lovers, and business associates time to think and adjust to things that may differ from their personal desires. At times, situations arise that require you to be diplomatic, considerate, and tactful. Do not force issues. You may have to compromise and do the little things that you overlooked last month. Use this month to cooperate with others while working on your projects, or help others with their ventures.

There are still some unresolved issues from last year that will need to be dealt with. You're in the process of closing matters that require termination— relationships, jobs, interests, outmoded beliefs. Be open-minded as you listen to others' sly remarks or constructive criticisms that may prove to be helpful. You may be overly sensitive and self-conscious, taking what others say the "wrong way" and end up with hurt feelings. Don't be that way. Try to be adaptable, understanding, and courteous while you wait for developments.

## February Vibrations (1 PY)

This month you will have an opportunity to feel happy, cheerful, playful, and self-expressive. This is a month to enjoy those friends you met in January, to entertain and be entertained. You'll have an active social life, there will be parties to attend, new and energetic people to meet. Situations will arise requiring you to have an attractive appearance and to put on a happy face. Call old friends you haven't talked to in awhile; take a phone number at a party and make a new contact. The friends you meet may open doors to new opportunities.

This is a good month to take a short vacation or to travel. Check out art shows or go to concerts with your friends. Shop for new clothes or decorate your home, but expect to lose money through frivolousness and extravagance. Leave your credit card behind. If you want to buy something on credit, ask yourself if you really need the item.

There are still be some endings looming in the background, waiting for conclusion. Watch for and avoid temper tantrums due to intense emotions and frayed nerves. If an ending presents itself, take the initiative to terminate the situation with a firm and determined attitude. Make use of your imagination to bring you to a positive conclusion.

Use this month to talk about your ideas, show off your talents, and have fun with friends, lovers, and coworkers. All forms of communication will be important. Express yourself using imagination, intuition, and inspiration in creative activities. Write, dance, paint, cook, or play a musical instrument.

Quite possibly you'll be led to a new opportunity in a creative direction. Approach a business opportunity with caution as it could develop differently than expected. Be creative and have fun.

## March Vibrations (1 PY)

This month, through hard work, you'll have an opportunity to produce substantial results and build for the future. The change that this year promises will begin to develop itself now. You must seriously apply yourself with regard to money, routines, and physical fitness. Organize yourself and your time to establish a solid foundation for future success.

You might have to take on more domestic responsibility. This month isn't the time to be lazy, disorganized, or impractical. Instead, you must use this month to reconstruct plans or projects and take care of any mistakes in finance or judgment. Think about creating a workable budget. Put everything in order to get ventures under way. Try not to be unreasonable or stubborn during contract negotiations. An inflexible attitude could hinder agreements, keeping opportunities from moving forward.

Situations will arise that demand a straightforward approach. Research your ideas and don't gamble on the unknown. At times, you'll probably feel very limited or restricted. It's important that you take time to analyze the limitations or restrictions and see whether they are of your own making. If so, plan to eliminate them. You might have to change your point of view and an "attitude adjustment" could be in store. Some limitations are unchangeable and you'll have to learn how to deal with them in a more satisfactory manner. Change your working conditions if you feel you need to, or change your rigid point of view.

Work instead of talking about what needs to be done. Be efficient and stabilize your finances. Follow through on commitments, organize time, and above all don't waste your energy. This is a time to throw silly notions out the window and be practical.

Although the month seems to be all work and no play, leave some time open for friends and family. If you need the support of others when the going gets rough, ask for it. You may feel a bit stressed, so remember to take care of your health. Sometimes just talking with a close friend or loved one about how you feel lightens the load significantly.

Next month you should see a change in your obligations and a break from the heavy workload.

## April Vibrations (1 PY)

This month you can expect a lot of activity, excitement, and an opportunity to expand your horizons, to progress, and make changes. You should get out and meet new people, see new places, experience new activities, and have unusual opportunities. Since there will be so many opportunities presenting themselves, and in many different areas, it might be difficult picking and choosing the one that's right for you. You will benefit by carefully focusing on the opportunity with the best potential for the future. You must realize that you can't handle every single opportunity that comes your way.

Too many irons in the fire will waste your time, money, and effort, leaving you with nothing permanent to hold on to. Focus on ideas that appeal to you. Try to keep ongoing ventures moving forward; don't forget about those projects that you worked on last month.

Whimsical ideas, travel, and a drive toward less responsibility are in the air. In fact, if you travel, you may find unusual or unexpected possibilities. Even though you may be out having a good time, keep an eye open to possibilities. ...

Be careful not to run yourself ragged and try to minimize responsibilities if you can, but don't ignore them. Without focus, you could tend to become unreliable, temperamental, and frustrated. Instead, practice self-discipline and you should come out ahead.

Watch legal commitments and expect conflicts and outbursts. Drop old, outmoded ways of thinking and acting and move forward with new ideas. Take a chance on luck and love, although love affairs may not last past August. Situations will arise requiring you to follow a hunch. If the odds are in your favor, take a chance. Be venturesome; try something different, spontaneous, dress to attract attention, and exercise. Unexpected possibilities are around every corner, so be flexible, resourceful, broad-minded, and full of energy to reap the rewards.

You may feel an excessive pull toward physical stimulation of the senses. Think twice before drinking and driving or spending all of your hard earned cash at the poker table. Consequences are always a part of every action. Constructive use of freedom is the key to making this a memorable month.

## May Vibrations (1 PY)

This month gives you an opportunity to pay attention to loved ones and home or community duties and responsibilities. This is your domestic month. You can enjoy sharing chores and good times with family or friends. Don't travel unless you're going to visit family. Be sure to maintain peaceful relationships, make domestic improvements, and be emotionally responsive.

The time is right to settle down, deepen love, and create harmony. Take time to enjoy children and to participate in children's activities. Keep your emotions in balance and show a great deal of affection. In fact, the more love you give, the more you will receive. This is a good time to enjoy the pleasures of romance, love, and marriage.

If you're married, rekindle your romance by taking advantage of special, loving and intimate interludes. If you're single, quite possibly someone you met last month could become a romantic interest. Or someone who suddenly ends up in your social scene might be the one you want to spend quiet times with.

At times, situations will arise that require you to sacrifice some of your personal desires, placing others' needs before your own. Use this month to be of service to your family, especially children. Take time to teach, pacify, and indicate approval. Through serving others you may find doors opening to new opportunities.

Change is in the air, and you may feel like making a significant shift in a family relationship. Be mature, devoted, and trustworthy when dealing with emotions. Becoming stubborn, intolerant, or worrying will cause stress and problems. Look to your inner feelings to guide you. Use your imagination and express yourself artistically—write, paint, cook, or play a musical instrument.

Thinking of remodeling, adding an addition to your home, or redecorating? Do whatever you can to make your home more comfortable and inviting. Perhaps it's time to make some changes in your yard. Begin by experimenting with different landscaping or gardening ideas. The focus on this month is to provide a peaceful, happy, and beautiful environment in your home.

### June Vibrations (1 PY)

This month gives you an opportunity to spend time alone, to analyze and clarify your goals, to learn from the past, and to plan for the future. So far, this year has brought many changes for you to think about and deal with. Now is the time to slow down and ponder what you've done thus far. You may enlist the aid of professionals (lawyers, therapists, counselors), or look into religious or metaphysical studies. It seems as though you're drawn to the unusual.

Instead of taking action this month, wait and analyze current legal dealings, questionable relationships, and future plans or goals. You should have a broad-minded, analytical, and critical point of view. Watch that you don't become too intellectual, thinking only from your mind, remember to use your heart, too. Think about what it is you want out of life and what you want to have happen during this year.

This month you seem to be on a different wavelength, and if you don't watch out you could alienate those who are close to you. It seems as though you want to spend more time alone, to read, study, research, write, teach, or enjoy philosophical conversations. Others may not understand or comprehend your desires. Pushing people away or creating arguments to gain time alone isn't productive. Make an extra effort at the beginning of the month to explain your need to spend some time by yourself. Try to make some time for family pursuits and spend time with loved ones so they won't feel totally neglected. Reassure your family and friends that by the end of the month you'll be ready for more company in your life.

This isn't the month to be aggressive, sociable, or to pursue commercial ambitions. Think before speaking and examine others' opinions carefully. Don't take what others say as gospel unless you are sure. Be a little secretive, and don't reveal your thoughts.

It will be best for you to wait for the telephone to ring instead of being the one to call. This month you must be patient, tolerant, and willing to spend time alone. If possible, spend some time in the country or change your diet and exercise. Go for long walks. You may learn something of significance for the future. Use this month to take care of your health. It's a good month to schedule medical and dental checkups.

### July Vibrations (1 PY)

This month gives you an opportunity to take control of business and financial matters. A dynamic time period for you to make a decisive move forward, heading to future success. You should rely on yourself, be forceful, self-confident, act decisively, approach matters in a businesslike manner, dress with dignity, and express yourself with authority. You will have more ability to make things happen with regard to business or financial matters than in any other month.

You'll have to make a major decision involving money. Watch that you don't overestimate your abilities and get yourself into something you can't handle financially. Make sure of any and all contracts and agreements before you sign on the dotted line. There may be a change or expansion in one of your ventures which has significant potential for the future.

Opportunities for advancement, recognition, financial improvement, and business expansion are there, but will only happen if you are organized, tactful, and persuasive. If you advertise and promote the projects you started eight or nine months ago, exceptional results will be achieved.

Associate with high-powered and enterprising people to help you take advantage of the opportunities. There's the likelihood of a new business opportunity presenting itself now. Perhaps this type of business has been an idea you've been formulating in the back of your mind all year and now here it is, at your fingertips. Be realistic, analyze and examine the situation from different perspectives and, if this is what you've been looking for, make your move. It's up to you to grab onto and seize important opportunities when they present themselves. Don't procrastinate.

Hard work and long hours may strain personal relationships. This isn't the time for vacations or undisciplined behavior. Forward thinking will pave the way for substantial success in business and financial matters.

## *August Vibrations (1 PY)*

This month gives you an opportunity to complete projects, be charitable, tolerant, and compassionate. You'll find the activities and fast pace of the previous months will begin to slow down; however, if you're working on projects or activities devoted to humanitarian causes, you'll be kept quite busy.

Use this month to help others, to be generous, kind, and inspire or counsel those who are in need of your support. You should try to give of yourself with little thought of reward. At times, situations will arise requiring you to have an unselfish, broad-minded attitude. Give blood, visit the elderly, needy, or sick and take a book, a treat, or a listening ear. This is a month for you to give of yourself.

Some of the projects, activities, or relationships that began eight or nine months ago are either completed or abandoned, causing you to readjust to different circumstances. The endings will likely be connected to much drama and strong emotions. Try to be understanding and compassionate regardless of the situation. It's best to handle differences with sensitivity and avoid quarrels if possible. This will be an emotional month, with strong feelings coming to the forefront. If a romantic relationship is ending, try to be understanding and compassionate while parting ways.

This isn't the time to begin anything new or to force your will on others. Take a long-distance trip if it's within your budget. This month can be used to meet with notable or helpful people who have the contacts or abilities to help further your ambitions.

Express yourself artistically, using your imagination, intuition, and inspiration for artistic creation. Write, paint, play a musical instrument, learn to cook a new dish. If you get out and promote yourself, your reputation may be enhanced by group interactions, auditions, and public appearances.

## September Vibrations (1 PY)

This month will be exciting and active. The time is right for forward movement and you should take the initiative. An important change may come into effect, bringing new solutions to some old problems. Developing new ideas or ventures may establish a major breakthrough in business. You'll be put in the driver's seat and it's up to you to act. Take care of the details and move forward. You may have to reschedule a family or social outing in order to work on your projects.

This month things get accomplished that were on the brink of completion three months ago but didn't materialize. The month is full of new people, situations, and ideas. Action is the keyword. Be aggressive and make changes. Don't procrastinate or become indecisive. Break up old conditions you don't like and strengthen weak areas. It's time to initiate a change that you may have been contemplating all year. Use originality and creativity, but don't go overboard and irritate or alienate others.

Base your decisions on independent and intellectual evaluations because you probably won't get any help or encouragement from others. The time is right for you to be yourself, emphasize your abilities, act independently and with self-confidence. You may end up seeing yourself differently.

It's also time for you to begin something new in other areas of your life: a new relationship, friendship, activity, vocation or hobby. This is a month for beginnings. Take a chance if the odds are in your favor.

## October Vibrations (1 PY)

Last month friends and family may have felt neglected. This month offers an opportunity for you to interact with friends and lovers and to make others happy. Rest and allow friends, lovers, and business associates time to think and adjust to things that may differ from their personal desires. At times, situations arise that require you to be diplomatic, considerate, and tactful. Don't force issues. Be sensitive to others feelings, especially your close friends and family. You may have to compromise and do the little things that you overlooked last month.

Although you feel the urge to act, this isn't the time to be ambitious or to make any material changes. Instead, this is a time for you to work quietly, to take care of the details that may slow you down later. You may experience delays in some of the ventures you began last month. Some delays may catch you by surprise and are out of your control. Wait patiently for developments, even though it may seem as though nothing is happening. The key to success this month is to learn patience and have faith that things are moving along. The timing isn't right at this particular moment, so don't waste time and energy forcing issues or trying to make things happen. If you push for results you could end up causing yourself more trouble at a later date.

Use this month to cooperate with others while quietly and calmly working on your projects. Help others with their ventures if you can. Be open-minded as you listen to others' sly remarks or constructive criticisms that may prove to be helpful. You may be overly sensitive and self-conscious, taking what others say the "wrong way" and end up with hurt feelings. Don't be that way. Try to be adaptable, understanding, and courteous while you wait for developments.

## November Vibrations (1 PY)

This month enjoy friends, entertain and be entertained. You'll have an active social life, getting together with friends in large or small gatherings. There will be parties to attend and energetic people to meet. Now is the time to spend with those people you've only seen sporadically during the busy year. Situations will arise requiring you to have an attractive appearance and to put on a happy face. Call old friends you haven't talked to in awhile; take a phone number at a party and make a new contact. The friends you meet may open doors to new opportunities. You might meet someone new who shares your creative or business interests. Perhaps this person is one with whom you'll form a valuable partnership.

This is a good month to take a short vacation or to travel. Shop for new clothes or decorate your home, but expect to lose money through frivolousness and extravagance. It's best to leave your credit card behind.

The projects you began four months ago will start to bloom, although not as quickly as you'd like. Delays are still possible, so continue using patience and faith that things will work out. Since this is a year of new beginnings, you might be presented with another new business opportunity. To get projects underway, use enthusiasm, imagination, and intuition.

Use this month to talk about your ideas, show off your talents, and have fun with friends, lovers, and coworkers. All forms of communication will be important.

Express yourself, using your imagination, intuition, and inspiration in creative activities. Write, dance, paint, cook, or play a musical instrument. Be creative and have fun!

## December Vibrations (1 PY)

This month, through hard work, you'll have an opportunity to produce substantial results and continue to build for the future. You must seriously apply yourself with regard to money, routines, and physical fitness. This month isn't the time to be lazy, disorganized, or impractical. Instead, you must use this month to reconstruct plans or projects and take care of any mistakes in finance or judgment. Put everything in order to get ventures under way. Situations will arise that demand a straightforward approach. Be sure to research your ideas and don't take chances on the unknown.

Although the holiday season is upon you and you'd rather spend time with friends and family, it's important that you don't neglect your obligations. Handle personal relationships with understanding and sensitivity.

At times, you'll feel very limited or restricted. It's important that you take time to analyze the limitations or restrictions and see whether they are of your own making. If so, plan to eliminate them. You might have to change your point of view and an "attitude adjustment" could be in store. Some limitations are unchangeable and you'll have to learn how to deal with them in a more satisfactory manner.

Work instead of talking about what needs to be done. You might have to take on more domestic responsibility. Be efficient and stabilize your finances. Review or revise your budget and stick to it. Follow through on commitments, organize time, and above all don't waste your energy. This is a time to throw silly notions out the window and be practical. You may feel a bit stressed, so remember to take care of your health. Try to make time for a physical or dental checkups.

# 2 PERSONAL YEAR VIBRATION

This will be a year to wait while last year's plans develop slowly; the ventures you began last year need time to fully mature. Be aware that you won't see results of last year's plans until next year. You'll find that developments will take longer than you first expected, causing you considerable frustration.

This is not the time to push to get your way. It will be important for you to understand that using extra effort to get things going won't make things happen any quicker and might even be detrimental to your growth, causing potential opportunities to disappear. In other words, "haste makes waste." This year, the worst that can happen is boredom.

Cooperation, patience, and harmony are the key words to your success. Try to keep in mind that you will progress more smoothly if you stay in the background and wait for developments, and that forcing issues will only cause problems. Delays and temporary stoppages might prove to be frustrating, but they could actually improve the ultimate timing needed for reaching your goals.

You'll learn the lesson of interdependence and will come to realize just how valuable you can be in a more passive role. Your ability and willingness to work with others will be tested and rewarded. You will find success by being cooperative, working in a partnership, and relating to others with tact and consideration. Although you may not be in a leadership role, you can still accomplish great tasks and may have the opportunity to further another's work with your time and effort.

You will begin to question some of last year's moves because there is a tendency now to analyze and rethink. After last year's planning, there are many details that need to be worked out. This year could bring a major shift in your life and you may have to make a decision about an important issue. This will be a year of integration, of putting new aspects into your old life. This year brings a time of unusual and strange experiences, extraordinary friendships, bizarre and sudden love affairs, a long distance trip, or a change of home and locality.

Be prepared for delays, detours, and postponements. Try not to get discouraged or anxious when things are blocked or seem to drag. Be patient. Situations and people may slow you down, but there is no hurrying this year. Don't worry, even if it seems nothing much is happening, it's just the inevitable slowing needed for new growth.

This year you'll find that your emotions and sensitivity seem to be at an all time high. You'll have to work to keep your emotions and sensitivity in balance. Many lessons will be learned about others and about yourself. Be aware of a tendency for extremes and don't let yourself be swayed by emotional depressions.

You may have difficulty with self-control which will increase nervous tension and generate disharmony. Save your nervous system by trying to avoid emotional intensity. Try to visualize yourself as others see you in order to realistically evaluate your strengths and weaknesses. You may have to learn patience in order to reduce the tension that's floating around in the air. Seek harmony with others. Above all, don't blame others when things don't go the way you want.

You will have a strong need for love and security. Watch out for emotional love affairs. If you are tactful, diplomatic, and not afraid to give of what you have—time, love, patience—this year should bring you new partnerships, new friendships, or the opportunity to cement a deep relationship with a person of the opposite sex. There is the possibility of marriage or separation, or the birth of a child. Unhappiness results if the relationship lacks in honesty, consideration, cooperation, or a desire to please. If truth is lacking, the relationship could come to an end. Cooperation with loved ones will bring about more happiness.

Be on the lookout for the possibility of being misled or cheated due to a lack of truth or honesty by others. Others may be dishonest or exaggerate. You may have to guard your territory against those trying to take over or interfering in your work, as partnerships and groups can bring both mutual advantage and problems. You may need to cooperate more and share the responsibilities with others. If you've made loans to people in the past, this year should see them repaying their debts.

The people who are offered for growth relationships this year will not be impressed by recklessness, impulsiveness, attention-getting power plays, aggressive behavior or immature attitudes. Watch that you don't get caught off guard due to nervousness or your headstrong action. This year you'll find that opportunities will come through others, making it important for you to be courteous. Focusing on details will encourage others to establish partnerships that will pay off in the future. Don't get caught up in trivial matters which could cause you to miss greater opportunities. You can advance in the world and improve your life as long as you make the effort to be wise and to try for something constructive.

Love, intimate friendships, and petty problems will strain emotional and physical energy, causing you to experience lowered vitality. Money comes in bits and pieces, little problems come in by the truckload, and delays get on your nerves. Plan times for rest, quiet, and meditation; take care of your health. Try to avoid becoming too sensitive, impulsive, and over-emotional.

Contemplation of your life will probably make you aware of your shortcomings as a human being, making you feel like a failure and becoming extremely self-conscious. It will be best for you to keep these feelings under control and to deal with self-doubt and your self-image constructively. Think things out calmly and guard yourself against self-pity. Self-discipline and self-control will bring a feeling of well-being and better health. Peace will come through meditation, spiritual thought, and prayer.

If possible, you should make improvements in your home, making it more attractive and comfortable. You could become frustrated because there will be many details to take care of in order for you to accomplish your desires. You will have to learn that getting the results you want will take time. This is a year to observe, refine, and be willing to keep the peace.

Listen to your intuition. This year you may find yourself equipped with greater powers of understanding, which makes you better able to adapt to changing circumstances. Since you are more intuitive, you may instinctively know how to react to change and how to gently advise people to go in the right direction. In fact, your role as confidant or advisor may be your key to success.

During the course of this year you may find out who your true friends are and how to be a real friend to others. Don't let petty annoyances cause major problems. Disruption of old ties can be very disturbing, causing misunderstandings and feelings of loss and separation. A lot of criticism and gossip may be directed toward you and there is no telling how justified this furor is. Face the temptation for retaliation and your own tendency for judgment of others. If you have spread rumors and criticism, the same conditions return now.

Avoid arrogance, rigidity, and stubbornness. If you become self-absorbed, insisting on your own priorities, you'll meet with much resistance. Try to work to avoid misunderstandings and build a cooperative spirit. Remain strong inwardly and try to be more flexible when dealing with others. If you keep the peace, cooperate, and live in harmony with others, you'll find your family and business conditions will improve considerably.

Become a true friend, loyal to family, friends and coworkers. People will seek you out for private talks once they sense your fine intuition, sensitivity and cooperative spirit. Allow yourself to be supported by friends and family. Share your deeper feelings with people you trust. You will find you have much to gain through socializing.

Last year was a year of independence, individuality, and beginnings. This year is one of cooperation, of learning that everyone around you is doing the best they can with their own unique energies. We all have a story to tell, and we are all equally important. This year, taking into account others feelings and the way we interact and treat each other will affect the quality of your life.

## Personal Month Vibrations (2 PY)

The following is a brief outline of the vibrations you can expect during the 2 Personal Year (for a more detailed description of what a specific month has in store for you, read the information found under the month heading, at the end of this section).

January through March bring new people and occasions to assist in your goals. Friends you met last November may advance your opportunities if they are not pressured.

During February you may experience a sense of frustration over small details, but you must put everything in order if you want to succeed. At times, you may feel held down by limitations or restrictions involving money, work, or family responsibilities. Analyze the limitations or restrictions and see whether they are of your own making. If so, eliminate them, or learn how to deal with them in a more satisfactory manner. Set some realistic goals. Agreements or associations may break up unless you are more than patient and considerate. During the early part of the year, make sure your roots are stable and growing and that all arrangements are accurate and carefully understood. There may be a conflict in a relationship and you will find love and sex don't always mix.

In March expand your horizons, but accept opportunities only if they don't disrupt your current plans or goals. You may find it hard to know what to do and could have difficulty in finishing what you start. Situations may arise requiring you to follow a hunch, but ignore long-shot possibilities.

April brings a chance to pay attention to loved ones, home or community duties and responsibilities. Situations will arise that require you to sacrifice some of your personal desires. It may seem as though everyone wants something from you, and you can't say no. Be mature when dealing with emotions.

In May you could be deeply disturbed about what others have said or done. For your own good, "snap out of it" and forget your self-importance for the time being. Try to cooperate. Above all, don't be mean as quarrels, separation, and unhappiness could result. If you feel depressed, meditation, reading, and study will bring you much peace. You may have to travel or be away from your mate for awhile.

Late spring and into July, things may become touchy and personal relationships will require attention. Money and power are the issues. Life may seem harder than you want, but if you work steadily, your efforts will pay off. You might get a small raise. Use your power to help others with their projects in a spirit of cooperation. You might want to sell something you've had for a long time.

July is a time to be discreet and learn. Don't push. There may be a completion of conditions as you could end some association or arrangement by necessity, or because of natural growth. Show compassion, understanding, and tolerance in your partnerships now; you may have to readjust to different circumstances. Don't begin anything new or force your will on others. Take a long-distance trip if it's within your budget.

From August to the end of the year, your deeper hopes and wishes should start to come to light if you have applied the knowledge and wisdom of this year's vibration. A change may come into effect, bringing new solutions to some old problems. The opening up of new arrangements, new living conditions and agreements should bring more peace of mind and satisfaction. You may start to see yourself differently.

Don't talk too much and try to keep things to yourself, especially during the autumn months. Although you feel frustrated waiting for developments, you must be patient while progress stays behind-the-scenes. Treat yourself and others well. Be loving, understanding, and sympathetic. Take time to do the little things you overlooked last month. Don't let nervous tension get the best of you. Be open-minded as you listen to others' sly remarks or constructive criticisms that may prove to be helpful.

In October, be generous in small ways, but don't splurge. Your verbal ability and imagination may be of considerable significance; use your sense of humor to your advantage. Creative talents and sensitivity may be used to quietly expand opportunities. All forms of communication will be important. You will have an active social life, with parties to attend and energetic people to meet. It's time to entertain and be entertained.

November brings a time to reorganize. Reorganize or renovate your home or job; take your clothes to the cleaners; file important papers; be careful with your money. Feelings of limitations or restrictions will be very strong. At times you may feel you are working so hard with little or no results. Resist the urge to be negative, stubborn, or angry when others seem to slack off. Stop using immature temper-tantrums to get your way.

December offers an opportunity to expand your horizons, and to make changes, although the changes may last only a couple of months. You may be tempted to have a love affair. Resist the temptation, especially if you or the other person are married. By the end of the year you should be able to see the difference between actions and reactions.

### January Vibrations (2 PY)

This month you will have an opportunity to feel happy, cheerful, playful, and self-expressive. This is a month to enjoy friends, to entertain and be entertained. You'll have an active social life, attending parties and meeting energetic people. Situations will arise requiring you to have an attractive appearance and to put on a happy face. The friends you meet may open doors to new opportunities, as long as they're not pushed. A friend may introduce you to someone who shares a common goal or has similar interests. Call old friends you haven't talked to in awhile; take a phone number at a party and make a new contact.

This is a good month to take a short vacation or to travel. Shop for the new clothes you've been wanting to buy, or decorate your home. Expect to lose money through frivolousness and extravagance, so it's best to leave your credit card at home. Buy only what you can afford.

The projects you began four months ago will start to bloom. Use this month to talk about your ideas, show off your talents, and have fun with friends, lovers, and coworkers. You'll benefit by offering to help others with their ventures; colleagues will be very appreciative of your efforts to assist them.

Take time to explore and develop some of your creative talents and abilities. Investigate different and exciting artistic activities. All forms of communication will be important. Express yourself, using your imagination, intuition, and inspiration in creative activities. Write, dance, paint, cook a new dish, or play a musical instrument. Just be creative and have fun!

### February Vibrations (2 PY)

This month, through hard work, you'll have an opportunity to produce substantial results and build for the future. You must seriously apply yourself with regard to money, routines, and physical fitness. This month isn't the time to be lazy, disorganized, or impractical. Instead, you must use this month to reconstruct plans or projects and take care of any mistakes in finance or judgment. Make sure you understand your contracts and agreements, and that legal paperwork is taken care of. Be patient as you put everything in order to get ventures under way. Act in a practical and down-to-earth manner. Situations will arise that demand a straightforward approach. Research your ideas and don't gamble on the unknown.

At times, you'll probably feel limited or restricted. It's important that you take time to analyze the limitations or restrictions and see whether they are of your own making. If so, plan to eliminate them. Some limitations are unchangeable and you'll have to learn how to deal with them in a more satisfactory manner. You might have to change your point of view. An "attitude adjustment" could be in store for you, which might be helpful if you find yourself bogged down in frustration.

You might find that you have to take on more domestic responsibility. Work instead of talking about what needs to be done. Be efficient and stabilize your finances, get started on a budget. Follow through on commitments, organize time, and above all don't waste your energy. Be sensitive and understanding in your all of your personal relationships.

Try to refrain from becoming impatient, wanting things to move along more quickly. Applying pressure to move things along will backfire on you. It's time for you to learn to accept circumstances and handle yourself in a mature, understanding manner. This is a time to throw silly notions out the window and be practical.

You may feel a bit stressed, so remember to take care of your health. Any problems associated with your health or well-being should be looked after promptly.

### *March Vibrations (2 PY)*

This month offers you an opportunity to expand your horizons, to progress, and make changes. Get out and meet new people, see new places, and experience new activities. Whimsical ideas and a drive toward less responsibility are in the air. In fact, if you take advantage of an opportunity to travel, you may find unusual or unexpected possibilities, along with some adventure. Try to minimize responsibilities if you can, but don't ignore them. Watch legal commitments and be prepared for conflicts and outbursts.

Take a chance on luck and love, although love affairs may not last. A romantic interest could spark your curiosity and then fade just as quickly as it started. Find time to get together with friends and family and enjoy being with each other. Be venturesome. Try something different, spontaneous, dress to attract attention, get out and do some exercising.

This is a month to drop your old, unproductive ways and look for new opportunities that can lead you in a positive direction. Situations will arise requiring you to follow a hunch. Take a chance if the odds are in your favor. Make sure that you examine new possibilities, checking them out thoroughly before you commit as they could promise a lot more than they actually deliver. Be careful not to run yourself ragged. If new opportunities don't progress of their own accord, you may want to think twice about whether you should continue the project. This isn't the month to get into risky propositions.

Don't lack focus, becoming unreliable, temperamental, immature, and frustrated. Unexpected possibilities are around every corner, so be flexible, broad-minded, and full of energy.

## April Vibrations (2 PY)
This month gives you an opportunity to pay attention to loved ones and home or community duties and responsibilities. This is your domestic month. It's not a time to travel unless you're going to visit family. You can enjoy sharing chores and good times with family or friends. This month be sure to maintain peaceful relationships, make domestic improvements, and be emotionally responsive.

This is an excellent time to enjoy the pleasures of romance, love, and marriage. In other words, the time is ripe to settle down, deepen love, and create harmony. Strong romantic feelings could have you thinking of cementing a deep relationship with someone close to you. Keep your emotions in balance and show a great deal of affection. In fact, the more love you give, the more you will receive.

Take time to enjoy children and to participate in children's activities. Share yourself with those close to you and celebrate good times together. You may be involved with young or old relatives and friends, some of whom may need your assistance. Use this month to be of service, taking time to teach, pacify, and indicate approval.

At times, situations will arise that require you to sacrifice some of your personal desires. Through serving others you may find doors opening to new opportunities. Be mature, devoted, and trustworthy when dealing with emotions.

Long-standing arguments or quarrels need to be addressed this month, bringing a resolution to old problems. Don't be stubborn, intolerant, or worrying. Give of yourself without thought of reward, nurture others, and act in a sensitive and loving way. Then step back and see how much better you feel about yourself and the world around you.

Use your imagination and express yourself artistically. Start to write, paint, cook something special, or play a musical instrument. Thinking of remodeling your home or garden? Go ahead and beautify your space. The focus on this month is to provide a peaceful, happy, and beautiful environment in your home.

### May Vibrations (2 PY)

This month you won't feel as social as you were last month, preferring to spend some quiet times to yourself. You want the opportunity to spend time alone, to analyze and clarify your goals, to learn from the past, and to plan for the future.

You'll seem to be drawn to the unusual. Enlisting the aid of professionals, such as lawyers, therapists, or counselors, or looking into religious or metaphysical studies may prove helpful. Study new material that relates to your present work.

You may learn something of significance for the future. Take time to be alone, read, study, research, write, teach, or enjoy philosophical conversations.

Instead of taking action this month, wait and analyze current legal dealings, questionable relationships, and future plans or goals. Reflect on what has transpired during the year, taking stock of the delays, which are likely to continue. Restore your faith that things are working behind the scenes and that all you need to do is wait patiently for things to progress. You should have a broad-minded, analytical, and critical point of view. Don't become too intellectual, thinking only from your mind. It will be important for you to remember to use your heart, too.

Friends and family members may feel neglected by your desire to spend time away from them. Instead of creating arguments or becoming annoyed with others, discuss your need to be alone with those close to you. Keeping your feelings under control might take an extra effort on your part. Instead of becoming irritated, try to be compassionate and understanding.

This isn't the month to be aggressive, sociable, or to pursue commercial ambitions. Think before speaking and examine others opinions carefully. Don't take what others say as gospel unless you are sure. Be a little secretive and try not to reveal your thoughts. Wait for the telephone to ring instead of being the one to call. This month you must be patient, tolerant, and willing to spend time alone.

If possible, spend some time in the country or change your diet and exercise. Go for long walks, get out in nature, listen to the birds. Take care of your health by scheduling medical or dental appointments.

### June Vibrations (2 PY)

You will have more ability to make things happen with regard to business or financial matters than in any other month. This month gives you an opportunity to take control of business and financial matters. You should rely on yourself, be forceful, self-confident, and act decisively. Approach all matters in a businesslike manner, dress with dignity, and express yourself with authority. Don't be overly aggressive or use your power the wrong way. Remain tactful and be especially considerate of your coworkers. If there are things that need to be changed in your business ventures, remember to inform associates so they don't feel left out.

It seems as though your business ventures are finally moving along and you can see some progress. You'll have to make a major decision involving money or finances. Don't procrastinate with decisions or take undue risks or chances. Take advantage of financial opportunities that you've researched and are totally clear about.

Associate with high-powered and enterprising people to help you take advantage of the possibilities. This isn't the time for travel or undisciplined behavior. Opportunities for advancement, recognition, financial improvement, and business expansion are there, but only happen if you are organized, tactful, and persuasive. If you advertise and promote the projects you started eight or nine months ago, exceptional results will be achieved.

Hard work and long hours may strain personal relationships. Try to schedule some time to spend with close friends and family. Taking a break now and then will rejuvenate your spirit.

## July Vibrations (2 PY)

This month gives you an opportunity to complete projects, be charitable, tolerant, and compassionate. Use this month to help others, to be generous, kind, and inspire or counsel those who are in need of your support. You should try to give of yourself with little thought of reward. At times, situations will arise requiring you to have an unselfish, broad-minded attitude. Give blood, visit the elderly, needy, or sick and take a book, a treat, or a listening ear.

The projects, activities, or relationships that began earlier are either completed or abandoned, causing you to readjust to different circumstances. You may have been waiting for some ventures to conclude themselves giving you the freedom needed to go on to the next step. However, there may be some relationships that you weren't expecting to end and this may come as a surprise you. The endings will likely be connected to much drama, strong emotions and feelings. Try to be understanding and compassionate regardless of the situation. Some family members or close friends may be overly sensitive, adding to your uncomfortable feelings.

If a personal relationship is nearing termination, you may experience strong passionate feelings. It's best to try to reign in your feelings, remain calm and take what comes with restraint and compassion. By the end of the month your strong feelings will have subsided and you'll begin to realize what happens is for the best. You will feel better about your self and your situation, having the weight of the past lifted from your shoulders.

This isn't the time to begin anything new or to force your will on others. Take a long-distance trip if it's within your budget. This month can be used to meet with notable or helpful people who have the contacts or abilities to help further your ambitions.

Express yourself artistically, using your imagination, intuition, and inspiration for artistic creation. Write, paint, play a musical instrument, learn to cook a new dish. Your reputation may be enhanced by group interactions, auditions, and public appearances.

## August Vibrations (2 PY)

This month will be active, and you should take the initiative. A change may come into effect, bringing new solutions to some of the problems you've been experiencing. You'll be put in the driver's seat and it's up to you to act. This month things get accomplished that were on the brink of completion months ago but didn't materialize.

This month is full of new people, situations, and ideas. It's time to start a new activity, friendship, or vocation. A new business associate or friend could enter your life who proves to be a genius with regard to helping you with your ventures. Be aggressive and make changes, breaking up old conditions you don't like and strengthening weak areas. You'll have to base your decisions on independent and intellectual evaluations because you won't get much help or encouragement from others.

Take a chance if the odds are in your favor. Be yourself and emphasize your abilities. You may end up seeing yourself differently. Use originality and creativity, but don't go overboard and irritate or alienate others. Continue to use diplomacy and tactful persuasion, as this is the only way you'll move your ventures forward, and gain the support of colleagues.

The bottom line for this month is: begin something.

## September Vibrations (2 PY)

This month offers an opportunity for you to interact with friends and lovers and to make others happy. Although you feel the urge to act on your business ventures, this isn't the time to be ambitious or to make any material changes. Instead, this is a time for you to work quietly, to take care of the details that may slow you down later. Wait patiently for developments, even though it may seem as though nothing is happening.

Try to keep this month calm and mellow. Rest and allow friends, lovers, and business associates time to think and adjust to things that may differ from their personal desires. At times, situations arise that require you to be diplomatic, considerate, and tactful. Don't force issues. You may have to compromise and do the little things that you overlooked last month. Use this month to cooperate with others while working on your projects, or help others with their ventures. Be open-minded as you listen to others' sly remarks or constructive criticisms that may prove to be helpful. You may be overly sensitive and self-conscious, taking what others say the "wrong way" and end up with hurt feelings. Don't be that way. Try to be adaptable, understanding, and courteous while you wait for developments.

Love and romance may be high on your list of priorities, and spending time with those close to you will be very important. This month could see you feeling closer to those you love, a sense of total commitment and togetherness pervades.

## October Vibrations (2 PY)

This month you will have an opportunity to feel happy, cheerful, playful, and self-expressive. This is a month to enjoy friends, to entertain and be entertained; there will be parties to attend, and energetic people to meet. You'll have quite an active social life. Throw yourself a party, invite your close friends, relatives, and don't forget about the children.

Situations will arise requiring you to have an attractive appearance and to put on a happy face. The friends you meet may open doors to new opportunities. Call longtime friends you haven't talked to in awhile; take a phone number at a party and make a new contact.

This is a good month to take a short vacation or for travel. Shop for new clothes or decorate your home, but expect to lose money through frivolousness and extravagance. It's best to leave your credit card locked up at home.

Watch that you don't scatter your energies, going off in all directions and accomplishing nothing. Wasting time isn't what this month is about. The projects you began four months ago will start to bloom. Keep your ventures moving ahead, taking care of the details, but try to take some time off for enjoyable activities. Use this month to talk about your ideas, show off your talents, and have fun with friends, lovers, and coworkers. All forms of communication will be important. Express yourself, use imagination, intuition, and inspiration in creative activities. Write, dance, paint, cook, or play a musical instrument. Whatever you do or become involved in make sure you enjoy yourself. Be creative and have fun.

### November Vibrations (2 PY)

This month, through hard work, you'll have an opportunity to produce substantial results and build for the future. You must seriously apply yourself with regard to money, routines, and physical fitness. This month isn't the time to be lazy, disorganized, or impractical. Instead, you must use this month to reconstruct plans or projects and take care of any mistakes in finance or judgment.

Put everything in order to get ventures under way. Situations will arise that demand a straightforward approach. Research your ideas and don't gamble on the unknown. Study legal documents, contracts and agreements thoroughly so you won't be caught unawares later. Negotiate the best deal for you.

There is the possibility you'll be buying or selling property, or building a home for yourself. This can be a big expense and requires logical and rational decision making skills. Keep an eye on your budget when making any decisions.

At times, you'll probably feel limited or restricted. It's important that you take time to analyze the limitations or restrictions and see whether they are of your own making. If so, plan to eliminate them. You might have to change your point of view. Maybe it's time for an "attitude adjustment." Know that some limitations are unchangeable and you'll have to learn how to deal with them in a more satisfactory manner. If you're bored with the job at hand, or find that it just doesn't seem to be going anywhere, realistically think about your options.

You might have to take on more domestic responsibility. Work instead of talking about what needs to be done. Take care of your obligations, and do the chores now so that they don't come back to haunt you at a later date. Be efficient and stabilize your finances. This is a time to throw silly notions out the window and be practical. Follow through on commitments, organize time, and above all don't waste your energy.

You may feel a bit stressed, so remember to take care of your health. Taking breaks now and then might be needed to relieve the pressures of the month.

## December Vibrations (2 PY)

This month will be eventful, offering you an opportunity to expand your horizons, to progress, and make changes. You should get out and accept invitations to meet new people, see new places, and experience new activities. There will be unusual opportunities around every corner. Whimsical ideas, travel, and a drive toward less responsibility are in the air. In fact, if you travel, you may find strange and unexpected possibilities. New and interesting opportunities seem to fall into your lap. Check them out for their potential. It seems as though you're in the right place at the right time.

Try to minimize responsibilities if you can, but don't ignore them. The delays and setbacks that hampered you for most of the year won't seem to bother you as much this month. Neglecting work and partying or socializing too much will cause problems.

During the festive season, don't take chances with drugs or alcohol. If you attend a party or a social outing, make sure you have a designated driver if you intend to partake in holiday cheer.

Take a chance on luck and love, although new love affairs may not last. Situations will arise requiring you to follow a hunch. If the odds are in your favor, take a chance. Be venturesome. Attempt something different, be spontaneous, dress to attract attention, and exercise.

Be careful not to run yourself ragged. It will be important for you to focus. If you don't, you'll become unreliable, temperamental, and frustrated. Watch legal commitments and expect conflicts and outbursts.

Unexpected possibilities are around every corner, so be flexible, broad-minded, and full of energy. Enjoy yourself and take advantage of every opportunity you get to meet new people.

# 3 PERSONAL YEAR VIBRATION

This year the focus is on creativity, new ideas, self-expression, and the joy of living. Life will offer opportunities for you to broaden your horizons, improve your old way of life, enjoy lighter interests, and socialize. You'll feel fresher and more alive than you have in previous years. It's important for you to be optimistic and cheerful. You can gain better results through being joyful and happy than through moods or worry. Realize that worry is just interest you pay for things that haven't happened yet.

Money, opportunity, travel, popularity, pleasure, happiness and love will be yours this year, but only through your own inspiration and good cheer. Scatter a little sunshine wherever you go. Create an atmosphere that attracts fun. This is a time for you to enjoy being alive.

You might find it harder to get things done, and you probably won't care so much if you don't. Try to overcome a tendency toward procrastination and put your best foot forward. Exercising self-discipline will be important. Do everything possible to improve yourself, particularly along the lines of your creative and artistic talents. This can be a year for writing, public speaking, acting, singing, sales, or media work. Now is the time to seek a market for your ideas. It might be wise to list your priorities and work on the ones you feel are most important.

You may have a lot of crazy ideas, sitting around with friends and dreaming up schemes to get rich, sell the house, buy a camper and travel. You feel different, more inspired and restless because your imagination is working so strongly now. Harness the dreams and visions which flash through your mind from time to time. If you don't focus you'll lose opportunities and creative urges on loose talk and socializing. Don't fall prey to gossip. Maintain self-discipline to avoid wasting time and energy.

Advancement or recognition in business, as well as friendship, is possible if you use your intuition, imagination and inspiration. Talk your ideas over with others to help you find the way, but don't be talked out of them. Think about your goals and try not to make important decisions unless you are absolutely convinced they are right.

This year can be unhappy if you drift along and want everything without effort, or allow yourself to be disturbed emotionally about what others do. Be careful not to exaggerate the importance of an unkind remark. What other people think of you is really none of your business.

Heightened emotions and sensitivity can cause problems and mood swings. This will be a volatile year and you'll need perspective. If you make a real effort to communicate and carry out some of your ideas in a constructive manner, this can be one of the happiest years of your life. Grab hold of something tangible, organize your time, and stick to the tasks at hand.

Since this is a year for pleasure, be sure to approach your experiences with joy, cheer and enthusiasm. Take time away from responsibilities to have fun. Get out with friends you enjoy spending your time with. Lead an active social life, lighten up, be social, take weekend trips, entertain, see movies, rent a sailboat, or go camping. Try to make new friends and join with the old ones, especially those who are doing worthwhile and creative things in the world. Get out of your rut! Look for ways to express yourself and enjoy life.

You'll find that there may be more than one outlet for your creative expression. Write letters, communicate, start a journal, and daydream. Friends and lovers may need a listening ear, so be ready with a joke, friendly advice, and a positive attitude. Be happy, gracious and eager to attract the people and experiences that will make this year important. If used properly, this can be a wonderful and memorable year. Exercise some restraint and caution yourself so you don't spread yourself too thin, scatter your energies, or spend all of your money.

You'll need to be appreciated and will enjoy admiring friends around. People will be drawn to you. Life will bring you new adventures and friends. Quite possibly people will begin to emerge from your past. The deep delights of love and happiness are offered with few strings attached. Friends and associates can open the door to business, fun and gifts.

For single persons there is the likelihood of being active with the opposite sex. It's important for you to handle your emotions constructively. Try not to be swept away by fantasies. You must be able to see people for who they really are. Sometimes this will be easier said than done. Don't be overly trusting; follow your gut reaction. Investigate the things people tell you instead of taking their words as gospel. Be content within yourself and your natural charm will be at its best.

This year, be careful to review what you say for unhappy problems could develop through talk, gossip, and careless speech. Disrespecting others and then justifying your actions won't do any good. Friendships can be ruined due to careless words or slips of the tongue. Take a look at yourself before you go pointing fingers at others. In fact, the next time you point a finger at someone notice that there are three fingers pointing back at you. You'll have to make some little sacrifices, but the love and appreciation you give will come back to you and you'll have much to be thankful for.

If you become too impulsive, having a desire to change the way things are, marital differences could escalate. Evaluate situations thoroughly and don't make any major decisions until you are sure. This year can bring out underlying emotional troubles as old or forgotten issues come to the surface. Try to release emotional blocks and work through problems.

You may be drawn into an unwise love affair, the eternal triangle. Even though your spouse, relatives, and family seem to be more difficult, think about the consequences of a careless action. Take into consideration what you might lose if you succumb to temptation. This year, the loss of friendship, especially the most intimate, can be damaging to your emotional nature. If a serious relationship ends you may turn to self-indulgent luxury, comfort, and superficial associations. Overspending, gossiping, extravagance or self-indulgence will hamper your progress, decreasing your chance of experiencing the pleasures this year offers. Instead, try to be there for others with a smile and a kind word.

If possible, try to take advantage of any opportunity to travel. You seem to have a strong desire to branch out, to do something completely different, and to better yourself both personally and financially. You'll find that travel will open doors for romance and business, bringing you happiness and popularity.

This is a time for you to enjoy life. Part of this year's purpose is to relieve tensions and burdens and to remind adults that the child within still lives. Take time to watch others entertain or to improve creative methods. Revive your interest in others and see how happy you can be.

Life can be beautiful. Don't fall prey to fearfulness or think that your dreams are unattainable. Self-defeating thoughts will only put a damper on the fun that this year has in store for you. This can be a playful and pleasurable year if you have the right attitude. Remember, true happiness comes from the inside. It's time to release those unhappy thoughts from the past and regain the happiness this year offers.

## Personal Month Vibrations in a 3 Personal Year

The following is a brief outline of the vibrations you can expect during the 3 Personal Year (for a more detailed description of what a specific month has in store for you, read the information found under the month heading, at the end of this section).

During the spring, make sure of your relationships and associations. Stay focused and remain on track, using good common sense. Don't allow yourself to detour. January will be very businesslike. Finish up some left over details from last year. You may have to ask friends for help with some of the work. Be efficient and don't overspend. Write down inspired thoughts or ideas that could very well pay off, at a later date.

February and March should activate social interests and bring intriguing people into your life. There is an indication of change and variety. You may experience a change in marital status or the amount of time you spend with your mate. Friends may bring conflicts. This is a good month for sales and promotion, but use caution and don't be too impulsive.

The focus for March is to provide a peaceful, happy and beautiful environment in your home. You will feel an urge to be creative and express yourself, but family needs have to be taken care of first.

April through June spend some time alone to pray, meditate, and organize things. Limit your projects so you have more quiet time. Friends may cause you some annoyance or emotional disturbances, but don't let this get you down. Try to understand your emotions and the things people do. Don't worry or fret about little things, especially about what others are doing. Be patient where money is concerned, as it may be slow in coming. Try not to make any major decisions in this unsettled time. Develop your creative talents and explore the possibilities of using your artistic or verbal talents this year.

If you work hard during May, some of your best plans will get a big boost. Use your imagination to take on a large project. Friends may unlock doors. It's advisable for you to associate with high-powered and enterprising people to help you take advantage of the opportunities. Watch what you buy and make sure you can really afford what you buy on credit. It might be wise for you to leave the credit card at home.

In June, learn to let go of your need to control and let situations unfold as they will. You may be easily influenced by what others say. Don't let others take financial advantage of you. Be generous, but businesslike or you could risk loss.

During the summer it is important that you put your best foot forward. New energy comes and now is the time to act. In July, take a trip or start a new line of work. This year there is a possibility you will have more than one job. Friends or social activities may create new opportunities for you. This could very well be one of the best times in years for creative breakthroughs, friendship, merriment, attracting a potential marriage partner, or fertility for hopeful parents.

During August, be happy and inspire people around you. Watch that you don't become over-sensitive. Listen to your intuition and follow your own guidance. Take time to study ways to improve yourself.

September can bring the opportunity to do what you want to do, with some friends helping. Force yourself to put in the extra effort if you lack motivation. You may be away from your mate for awhile. Attend trade shows or markets. Old and new relationships should be encouraged. Talk may be all that is accomplished until October, but the plans and ideas for discussion will bring in work and tangible assets for the following year.

October brings a glimpse of what next year will be like—hard work and feelings of frustration. Learn how to analyze and deal with limitations and restrictions that are unchangeable or see whether they are of your own making. You'll find that things will improve if you change your point of view.

November could possibly be an explosive time, expect surprises and a clash of wills. Your energy should be high, making you attractive to others. There is the possibility you may meet someone with whom you will have an important and meaningful relationship. Watch an excessive appetite for physical stimulation. Don't eat or drink too much, take drugs, or go overboard on sex. Learn from past mistakes instead of repeating them. Legal troubles could result if you are careless, or act irresponsibly.

December carries pleasure, but responsibilities too. Domestic duties may feel restrictive, but try to be of service, to teach, pacify, and indicate approval. The special, little things you say and do will go a long way when dealing with those close to you. If single, you may be fantasizing about marriage now, but wait until next February to make any decisions. Watch for too much emotional feeling and don't allow emotions to rule your actions.

## January Vibrations (3 PY)

Through hard work, you'll have an opportunity to produce substantial results and build for the future. If you take care of the tasks that come your way this month you'll get the year started off in the right direction. You must seriously apply yourself with regard to money, routines, and physical fitness. This month isn't the time to be lazy, disorganized, or impractical. Instead, you must use this month to reconstruct plans or projects and take care of any mistakes in finance or judgment. Put everything in order to get ventures under way. Some friends may provide assistance with your projects if they are approached tactfully.

Situations will arise that demand a straightforward approach. Research your ideas and don't gamble on the unknown. At times, you'll probably feel limited or restricted. It's important that you take the time to analyze the limitations or restrictions and see whether they are of your own making. If so, plan to eliminate them. You might have to change your point of view, an "attitude adjustment" could be what's needed. Some limitations are unchangeable and you'll have to learn how to deal with them in a more satisfactory manner. Flying off the handle won't get you anywhere. Keep emotions in check when dealing with others or you could appear immature.

You will have to take on more domestic responsibility. Work instead of talking about what needs to be done. This is a time to throw silly notions out the window and be practical. Be efficient and stabilize your finances. It's a good idea to create a realistic budget for the year. Follow through on commitments, organize time, and above all don't waste your energy.

Quite possibly you'll be entertaining the thought of buying or selling a house or property. Make sure all legal paperwork is thoroughly scrutinized and your "ducks are in a row."

You may feel a bit stressed, so remember to take care of your health. If something is wrong or you don't feel quite right, make an appointment for a checkup. By the end of the month you should feel more relaxed and ready to socialize with friends and relatives.

### February Vibrations (3 PY)
This month offers you an opportunity to expand your horizons, to progress, and make changes. You should get out and meet new people, see new places, experience new activities, and have unusual adventures. At times you may have a variety of new opportunities to choose from and, with so much going on, it will be difficult for you to figure out what it is you really want. It's best to avoid acting on impulse. Slow down for a moment and think. Exercise caution in new ventures and steer clear of frivolity. Some ventures you begin now need time to grow.

Whimsical ideas, travel, and a drive toward less responsibility are in the air. In fact, if you travel, you may find unusual or unexpected possibilities presenting themselves. Try to minimize responsibilities if you can, but don't ignore them. You'll most likely feel freer than you have in a long time.

Take a chance on luck and love, although new love affairs may not last. Watch the commitments you make. Expect conflicts and outbursts if you don't follow through on your promises. Be careful not to run yourself ragged. Don't lack focus, becoming unreliable, temperamental, and frustrated. Take time to spend special moments with your spouse or lover, including children when the activity is appropriate for youngsters.

Situations will arise requiring you to follow a hunch. If the odds are in your favor, take a chance. Be venturesome and try something different, spontaneous, and dress to attract attention. Begin a new exercise regimen. Drop old unproductive habits and behaviors. Look for something new. Unexpected possibilities are around every corner, so be flexible, broad-minded, and full of energy.

## March Vibrations (3 PY)

This is your domestic month, a time for you to pay attention to loved ones and home or community duties and responsibilities. Don't travel unless you're going to visit family. Be sure to maintain peaceful relationships, make domestic improvements, and be emotionally responsive. The time is right to settle down, deepen love, and create harmony. You can enjoy sharing chores and good times with family or friends. Take time to enjoy children and to participate in children's activities.

If you've had a difference of opinion with some family members (parents, siblings, or other close relatives), now is the time to try and resolve the problem. Be mature, devoted, and trustworthy when dealing with emotions. Don't be stubborn, intolerant, or worrying. Use your imagination to help you figure out how to resolve your differences. Try to create peace and harmony with loved ones. Keeping your emotions in balance and showing a great deal of affection will work wonders. In fact, the more love you give, the more you will receive.

This is a good time to enjoy the pleasures of romance, love, and marriage. At times, situations will arise that require you to sacrifice some of your personal desires. Use this month to be of service. Find time to teach, pacify, and indicate approval. Through serving others you may find doors opening to new opportunities. Even though family obligations may seem never ending, taking time for the pursuit of happiness with those close to you will bring great reward.

Make some time to use your imagination and express yourself artistically. Write, paint, cook, or play a musical instrument. The focus on this month is to provide a peaceful, happy, and beautiful environment in your home.

*April Vibrations (3 PY)*

This month gives you an opportunity to spend time alone, to analyze and clarify your goals, to learn from the past, and to plan for the future. What is it you want to accomplish this year? Instead of taking action this month, wait and analyze current legal dealings, questionable relationships, and future plans or goals. You should have a broad-minded, analytical, and critical point of view. But watch that you don't become too intellectual, thinking only from your mind. Remember to use your heart, too.

You may enlist the aid of professionals or look into religious or metaphysical studies. You'll seem to be drawn to the unusual. This is also a time to take stock of some of your personal problems and to think about changing unproductive attitudes that hinder your progress. You may have a spiritual awakening or a new awareness.

This isn't the month to be aggressive, sociable, or to pursue commercial ambitions. Think before speaking and examine others opinions carefully. Don't take what others say as gospel unless you are sure. Be a little secretive and don't reveal your thoughts. Take time to be alone. Read, study, research, write, teach, or enjoy philosophical conversations.

At times you may have to explain your desire to spend time by yourself to others who might feel neglected or left out. Don't cause disagreements or fights with loved ones to gain space for yourself. Discuss your needs to alleviate any annoying or resentful feelings.

Wait for the telephone to ring instead of being the one to call. This month you must be patient, tolerant, and willing to spend time alone. If possible, spend some time in the country or change your diet and exercise. Go for long hikes in the woods or take quiet walks in nature. You may learn something of significance for the future when you let your mind wander. Take care of your health when you can or if you feel there is a problem.

*May Vibrations (3 PY)*

This month gives you an opportunity to take control of business and financial matters. You should rely on yourself, be forceful, self-confident, act decisively, and approach matters in a businesslike manner. When out and about or meeting potential clients, dress with dignity and express yourself with authority. You will have more ability to make things happen with regard to business or financial matters than in any other month.

You'll have to make a major decision involving money. Whatever you do, don't procrastinate. Opportunities for advancement, recognition, financial improvement, and business expansion are there, but only happen if you are organized, tactful, and persuasive. Associate with high-powered and enterprising people to help you take advantage of the opportunities.

A close friend or associate could provide you with an interesting solution to consider regarding a business problem. Imagination will prove helpful in business ventures. If you advertise and promote the projects you started eight or nine months ago, exceptional results will be achieved. Hard work and long hours may strain personal relationships. It will be important for you to try and schedule a little time for social activities. This isn't the time for vacations or undisciplined behavior; however, business travel may provide a little break from the routine.

## June Vibrations (3 PY)

This month gives you an opportunity to complete projects, be charitable, tolerant, and compassionate. Use this month to help others, to be generous, kind, and inspire or counsel those who are in need of your support. You should try to give of yourself with little thought of reward. At times, situations will arise requiring you to have an unselfish, broad-minded attitude. Give blood, visit the elderly, needy, or sick and take a book, a treat, or a listening ear.

The projects, activities, or relationships that began eight or nine months ago are either completed or abandoned, causing you to readjust to different circumstances. Using creativity to complete a project now will pave the way for new work later.

This month endings will likely be connected to much drama and strong emotions, especially if a friendship is drawing to a close. Try to be understanding and compassionate regardless of the situation. Keeping your feelings in check and taking into consideration how the other person feels may take extra effort on your part. It's up to you to exercise your understanding, tolerance, and compassion. This isn't the time to begin anything new or to force your will on others. Let the experience end on a positive note if you can. Realize that conclusions make way for regeneration and new freedoms.

Take a long-distance trip if it's within your budget. This month can be used to meet with notable or helpful people who have the contacts or abilities to help further your ambitions. You may meet someone new with whom you'd like to begin a romance. Romantic interludes, although welcome and enjoyable, will be short lived, fading as quickly as they started.

Express yourself artistically, using your imagination, intuition, and inspiration for artistic creation. Write, paint, play a musical instrument, learn to cook a new dish. Your reputation may be enhanced by group interactions, auditions, and public appearances.

## July Vibrations (3 PY)

This month will be active, and you should take the initiative. A change may come into effect, bringing new solutions to some old problems. You'll be put in the driver's seat and it will be up to you to do something constructive. In fact, you'll feel like going full steam ahead with some of your projects.

This month things get accomplished that were on the brink of completion three months ago but didn't materialize. Remind yourself that you must remain focused because if you act impulsively you could lose out on an excellent opportunity. Be aggressive and make changes. Break up old conditions you don't like and strengthen weak areas. Base your decisions on independent and intellectual evaluations because you probably won't get any help or encouragement from others. You may even begin to see yourself differently.

Take a chance if the odds are in your favor. Use originality and creativity, but don't go overboard and irritate or alienate others. Your verbal skills will be important; try not to use your words as swords or you could end up regretting things you've said.

This is a month for beginnings, full of new people, situations, and ideas. Start a new activity, friendship, or vocation. Be yourself and emphasize your creative abilities. Show others how happy and joyful you can be.

## August Vibrations (3 PY)

This month offers an opportunity for you to interact with friends and lovers and to make others happy. Although you feel the urge to act, this isn't the time to be ambitious or to make any material changes. Instead, this is a time for you to work quietly, to take care of the details that may slow you down later. Although you may be busy, experiencing a great deal of activity with regard to your projects, there will also be some down time. Wait patiently for developments, even though it may seem as though nothing is happening.

Rest and allow friends, lovers, and business associates time to think and adjust to things that may differ from their personal desires. At times, situations arise that require you to be diplomatic, considerate, and tactful. Don't force issues. You may have to compromise and do the little things that you overlooked last month.

Use this month to cooperate with others while working on your projects, or help others with their ventures. The assistance you give to friends or associates will be appreciated and will come back to you when you need help at a later time. Share the spiritual insights you may have. Spreading good thoughts and cheer will delight others.

Be open-minded as you listen to others' sly remarks or constructive criticisms that may prove to be helpful. You or a close friend may be overly sensitive and self-conscious, taking things the "wrong way" and ending up with hurt feelings. It's best if things that were said are discussed calmly in order to reach an understanding, taking into consideration each other's feelings. If not, progress will be hampered by resentful feelings. This month it's best for you to try to be adaptable, understanding, and courteous while you wait for developments.

## September Vibrations (3 PY)

This month will be very exciting and socially active. Situations will arise requiring you to have an attractive appearance and to put on a happy face. You'll have an opportunity to feel happy, cheerful, playful, and self-expressive. Enjoy friends, entertain and be entertained. You'll be invited to parties or other social functions, and will have the chance to meet up with longtime friends you haven't seen in awhile. There is the possibility of meeting some new and energetic people, too. Take a phone number at a party and make a new contact because the friends you meet may open doors to new opportunities.

This is a good month to take a short vacation or to travel on the spur of the moment. Shop for new clothes and decorate your home. If you become frivolous and extravagant you could lose money, so think about what you buy. It might be a good idea to leave your credit card at home instead of in your wallet.

The projects you began four months ago will start to come to fruition. Use this month to talk about your ideas, show off your talents, and have fun with friends, lovers, and coworkers. All forms of communication will be important. Express yourself by using your imagination, intuition, and inspiration in creative activities. Go to a concert, open your mind to new and different music. Write, dance, draw, cook, play a musical instrument, or explore singing and acting. This is a time to be creative and have fun. So do it!

## October Vibrations (3 PY)

This month, through hard work, you'll have an opportunity to produce substantial results and build for the future. You must seriously apply yourself with regard to money, routines, and physical fitness. This month isn't the time to be lazy, disorganized, or impractical. Instead, you must use this month to reconstruct plans or projects and take care of any mistakes in finance or judgment. Put everything in order to get current ventures under way. Situations will arise that demand a straightforward approach. Research your ideas and don't gamble on the unknown.

At times, you'll probably feel limited or restricted by a heavy workload. It's important that you take time to analyze the limitations or restrictions and see whether they are of your own making. If so, plan to eliminate them. You might have to change your point of view or your attitude about a problem. Some limitations are unchangeable and you'll have to learn how to deal with them in a more satisfactory manner. This is a time to throw silly notions and excuses out the window.

Be enthusiastic as you take on more domestic responsibility. Do the work instead of complaining or talking about what needs to be done. Look for ways to be efficient and to stabilize your finances. Don't make promises you have no intention of keeping. It is important for you to follow through on commitments and organize your time. Above all don't become scattered, going off in all directions and wasting your energy.

You may feel a bit stressed, so remember to take care of your health. Throw a party or go to one when you need to take a break. Spread sunshine and joy wherever you go and you'll end up feeling happier about yourself and others.

## November Vibrations (3 PY)

Another social month arrives as November offers you an opportunity to expand your horizons, to progress, and make changes. You should get out and meet new people, see new places, experience new activities, and have unusual opportunities. Unique ideas, travel, and a drive toward less responsibility are in the air. If you travel, you may find fantastic or unexpected possibilities. Try to minimize responsibilities if you can, but don't ignore them. In fact, if you decide to take care of some work obligations instead of escaping into the physical senses, you'll be in a much better position when next year arrives.

Watch legal commitments and expect conflicts and outbursts. Exercise self-discipline while socializing with friends and family. If you drink and drive, you'll get to experience the inside of a jail cell. Restlessness and impulsiveness leads to running yourself ragged. Scattering your energies in all sorts of different directions will only cause frustration. It will be important for you to focus on positive enterprises so you don't become unreliable, temperamental, and frustrated. Keeping a sense of balance and proportion in whatever you do will make life flow a lot easier.

Take a chance on luck and love, although love affairs may not last. Situations will arise requiring you to follow a hunch. If the odds are in your favor, take a chance. Be venturesome, try something different, spontaneous, dress to attract attention, and exercise. Drop what doesn't work for you and look for something new. Unexpected possibilities are around every corner, so be flexible, broad-minded, and full of energy.

## December Vibrations (3 PY)

This month gives you an opportunity to pay attention to loved ones and home or community duties and responsibilities. This is your domestic month, a good time to enjoy the pleasures of romance, love, and marriage. This isn't the month to travel unless you're going to visit family members. Spending time with close friends and relatives will prove to be extremely satisfying as the year comes to a close. Make every effort to maintain peaceful relationships, make domestic improvements, and be emotionally responsive.

The time is right to settle down, deepen love, and create harmony. During part of the month you can enjoy sharing chores with your loved ones as you get your home ready for the holidays. Enjoy children and participate in their activities. Keep your emotions in balance and show a great deal of affection. In fact, the more love you give, the more you will receive.

At times, situations will arise that require you to sacrifice some of your personal desires and you will be asked to be of service to others. Give of yourself without thought of reward. Take time to teach, pacify, and indicate approval. Through serving others you may find doors opening to new opportunities. Be mature, devoted, and trustworthy when dealing with emotions. Don't be stubborn, intolerant, or worrying. Worry doesn't do you any good anyway.

If possible, use your imagination and express yourself artistically by writing, painting, cooking, or playing a musical instrument. The focus on this month is to provide a peaceful, happy, and beautiful environment in your home.

# 4 PERSONAL YEAR VIBRATION

At the beginning of the year, it will be necessary for you to give some time to seriously thinking about the future. If you plan well, ideas can be worked out enabling you to gain much in the way of security and future stability. This is a building year. A time for you to lay down a firm foundation with regard to building home, family, and business.

The 4 Personal Year may seem long and hard. It's definitely a year full of work, hard work, most of the time. This down-to-earth year will allow you to correct some of the material mistakes you've made in the past. In order to succeed, you'll have to keep your nose to the grindstone and not look for easier paths or ways of getting out of doing the work that's required of you. This is a year for you to persevere, save, and start accumulating some assets.

It's time for you to pay attention to a basic routine and a heavy work schedule. The positive note here is that you can expect to see results for all of your efforts and will finally begin to see some material rewards for the projects you started three years ago. Putting forth the effort now will help stabilize your life over the next five years.

You probably won't find much time for personal pleasure and will have to rely on last year's variety of interests and friendships to bring in some social activity. You may have to forgo vacations, party times, or unscheduled expenditures. You'll have to go against your natural tendencies to want to play instead of work. Learning how to budget, to take care of home, family and business, will bring rewards.

There will be times when conditions seem slow and you'll feel held down, frustrated and restricted. It will be important for you to realize that feelings of limitation or restriction often grow from your point of view rather than from the work itself. You'll have to face situations as they really are, not by how you want them to be. Remember that results will be accomplished if you take the responsibility. The key word during this year is balance.

This is a year for you to keep an eye on future payoffs. A time to buy, sell, or trade, and for all activities concerned with building homes, property, and laying a solid and practical foundation for the future. If you have the money, invest in real estate, landscape your yard, build a fence, buy a new house, or repair the roof on an old one.

There will be times you'll be forced to look at things from a material point of view and to stay on the job whether you feel like it or not. More often than not, you won't feel like it, wanting instead to take the easy way out. Discipline yourself because if you work hard, by the time the year is over, you'll feel considerable satisfaction in the things you've accomplished. Keep these thoughts in the back of your mind and call upon them at times when you need to keep focused on what you're doing. Hard work will pay off.

This year it will also be very important for you to manage your finances, career, work, and home. Face the facts and get down to business in order to lay a solid foundation for future development and security. You must be organized, have a plan or goal, and manage all of your affairs constructively.

In matters pertaining to business, property, agreements, contracts, or legal affairs, details will have to be attended to with patience and honesty. It's important for you to know the facts and above all, don't take undue risks. Don't put your trust in luck or allow yourself to be careless. Thoroughly research ideas or opportunities that come your way through the thoughts and minds of other people. Proceed only when you are sure the ventures are of a sound nature and will pay off.

Finances are going to seem slow, and expenses will be high. You'll feel very limited and restricted with regard to time and money. Use good common sense to meet all of the obligations and requirements and you will come out ahead. Before you pull out your credit card, truthfully ask yourself if you really need the item. Then put the credit card back in your wallet and wait for a day when you can afford to pay with cash.

This year, you'll feel the need to calm down, get settled, organize, follow a routine, take responsibility, and to see things through. You may have to watch a tendency to create your own version of reality. Curb your tendency to daydream and go off in all directions.

It's time to concentrate on mending and repairing. You will be dealing with relatives, in-laws, old friends, property, landscaping and lawn maintenance. Others will tend to be demanding of your time and money and you will be required to make some sacrifices. Try to avoid needless quarrels and misunderstandings.

Since your own opinions seem to be stronger and your attitude is less than relaxed, you might find yourself doubting others and becoming more critical or judgmental of their lifestyles. Others may find you uncommunicative which can create distance between you and your loved ones. It's best for you to try and work through difficult relationships instead of flying off the handle or becoming stubborn. To get the best this year has to offer, you'll have to be patient, cool-headed, and practical. And, if you make promises, remember to keep them.

Avoiding work or evading the responsibility won't do you any good. In fact, if you don't take the initiative and do what's required of you this year, you'll regret it later and will find the obligations you've shirked still present when next year comes along. Each year brings its own requirement and opportunity for growth and prosperity, this is your work-hard-year, next year is your year for freedom.

Even though this may seem like a difficult year, there will be times for pleasure with friends and family. All work and no play isn't what the year intends for you. This year you'll benefit by saving money and being constructive. It's important for you to remember that you won't always be feeling so limited, restricted and serious. If you prepare yourself, you'll be able to take advantage of vacations, sensual pleasures, adventure, and the chance to break from routine next year. Although there will be many problems, there is a promise that by the end of the year you'll experience a sense of accomplishment.

If you work at something you have already done, you may find yourself becoming bored or feeling confined. This could be a good time for you to look for opportunities that offer new challenges. You may have to go on short business trips, spending some time away from your family, causing a strain in your love relationship.

Locked-up emotions will have to be dealt with openly and honestly. Expressing your feelings may be difficult, and you'll have to learn to share feelings with your loved ones. Although it may be difficult for you, discussing problems will prove beneficial in the long run. Sometimes, by getting your burdens out in the open, the solutions become clearer to you. You will find that little is gained by escaping the situation. It's time for you to clarify any real or self-imposed limitations or restrictions, change your opinions, form a new attitude towards life, and test the value of plans. Make a goal book, it really does work.

In order for you to take advantage of situations and make the most of options open to you, you'll be required to show self-discipline, moderation, and endurance. Careful planning, creating and following a budget, conscientiousness, and a business-like attitude are required. The people who are working behind the scenes and who are there to aid in your growth are practical problem-solvers who won't appreciate incompetence, childish behavior, or frivolity. You may have to use their input to adopt a different point of view and to recognize the inevitable.

You'll attract supporters if you show them you are reliable, trustworthy, dedicated to your work, faithful, and have a positive attitude. If you do the work at hand, you may be given more responsibility, or recognized for past achievements in business, which might come as a surprise to you.

In order for you to cultivate long-term goals, you'll have to be sane and rational in all of your endeavors. It's time to correct misconceptions. Take care of your finances and, if possible, try to terminate old debts. Think about conditions as they really are and find ways to get things under control. Do the work and take responsibility. Remember, this is a year for building. Build your business, your home, and your family on solid ground.

## Personal Month Vibrations in a 4 Personal Year

The following is a brief outline of the vibrations you can expect during the 4 Personal Year (for a more detailed description of what a specific month has in store for you, read the information found under the month heading, at the end of this section).

At the beginning of the year, write down your goals, map out a plan and a routine and stick to it. January will start off with such an increase of activity and opportunity that it'll seem like you'll be in the top job or on cloud nine by the end of the year. Watch some of the decisions you made last December as they will likely change. You'll feel restless, wanting things to move quicker than they are. Have patience. You may be prompted to make important changes or decisions in your living arrangements due to a need to control your environment or to settle down. You'll find that opportunities are misleading as much more work will be required than is apparent.

February is the best month for personal relationships. Love and romance will be important, but will have a tendency to cause your emotions to sway. You will have to work to keep feelings balanced. You may be surprised by an unexpected show of love and affection from an admirer. Don't go making promises you can't keep.

Watch your emotions from March through May, as things seem to fall apart at the seams either on the personal, business, or emotional level. Important people are watching you behind the scenes, so be careful not to let your performance slip. At times you may feel like throwing in the towel and giving up. If your actions are mature and responsible, you may be able to salvage your position or negotiate a new one.

Troubles with your spouse or personal relationship start to surface and will have to be dealt with. It's time to ferret out locked-up emotions. You'll have to work at expressing your feelings and to share feelings with loved ones. You won't gain anything by escaping the situation. Money prospects will be slow in coming, adding to your feelings of limitation and restriction.

In March, make time to take care of your health and schedule checkups. Try to take quiet breaks and don't become a workaholic. Use coffee or lunch breaks to walk around outside for a few minutes, stop for a moment and take a deep breath.

April will be an excellent month for major purchases, buying property, or promoting yourself and your abilities. You'll have excellent judgment. Avoid risks or long-shot possibilities. If you advertise and promote the projects you began earlier, exceptional results will be achieved.

By late spring you will be faced with some conclusions. During May, a relationship (business or personal) may require a lot of your attention or it could come to an end. You'll have to be prepared to deal with strong emotions and feelings. It's best to realize that some things are beyond your control. Trust that the Universe will bring you what you need. You may have to travel and spend some time away from your family.

June brings some decisions to make and a new trend of events. It's time for you to take pride in your accomplishments. You could be starting a new business; have the opportunity to work out of your home, get married, have a baby. If you want to increase your independence, you'll have to work hard to break up the old conditions and strengthen the weak areas.

From June on, decisions will be crucial as things are about to happen which can open some very important doors in your career. It's time for you to do a little self-evaluating and scrutinizing if you find you're dissatisfied or haven't improved your working environment. Be willing and able to see what is in you that may have caused you to miss opportunities. Progress will probably be difficult for you to see and you'll feel an increase of nervous tension which will add to the restrictive feelings.

August offers the first break from the hard work and pressure since the beginning of the year. Travel, do some shopping, hang out with your friends, or decorate your home. Try and take time to enjoy yourself now because September will be very difficult.

September will bring a harshly restrictive work load and many practical problems for you to handle. Housework will seem to get out of control; your career will demand more of your time and effort. Lots of hard work is in store for you and there's no getting around it. Keep your eyes on the future even though you feel very limited and restricted now. Remember you're building a foundation for the future and through hard work you'll have an opportunity to produce substantial results. You'll find you can learn a lot through obstacles and challenges, as long as you have the right attitude. Learn from past mistakes and make an effort not to repeat them.

October brings a glimpse of the activity and change that next year will bring. But, remember you still have a lot of work to do, and if you neglect your work now, you will regret it later. You may be tempted to have an affair. Resist the temptation. Love triangles will only upset you and cause you more problems. Don't expect things to go the way you thought they would or the way you planned.

In November, spend time with your family and enjoy the domestic side of life. Peaceful relationships may be difficult and you'll be required to put forth considerable effort to make domestic improvements and be emotionally responsive. You'll either feel secure or trapped. Watch your promises and follow through.

The holiday season allows for some time to slow down and think. Because you'll start to feel the vibrations of next year, work and planning may feel restrictive. Don't fight circumstances. Demand less of your mate and children. You'll probably find that your finances are less than desired. Unless you have a popular specialty, December will be a poor month for money. It will be important for you to stay balanced and have faith, for now is the time you'll experience the reward for the hard work done during the year.

## January Vibrations (4 PY)

This month is active and offers you an opportunity to expand your horizons, to progress, and make changes. You should get out and meet new people, see new places, experience new activities, and have unusual opportunities. Whimsical ideas, travel, and a drive toward less responsibility are in the air. In fact, if you travel, you may find unusual or unexpected possibilities.

Try to minimize responsibilities if you can, but don't ignore them. Watch legal commitments and expect conflicts and outbursts. You will need to exercise caution when choosing or participating in certain activities. Illegal activities will have consequences. Take a chance on luck and love, although love affairs may not last.

Situations will arise requiring you to follow a hunch. If the odds are in your favor, take a chance. Be venturesome, but realize that a new venture could end up being misleading, requiring more work to get it off the ground than you originally thought. Try something different, spontaneous, dress to attract attention, and exercise.

Dropping the old and looking for the new may be what you feel like doing, but realize that existing ventures might still have some potential. It might be advisable to wait until you get more information before you determine the right course of action to take. Patience might not be something you have in abundance right now. Be careful not to run yourself ragged. Don't lack focus, becoming unreliable, temperamental, and frustrated. Unexpected possibilities are around every corner, so be flexible, broad-minded, and full of energy.

## February Vibrations (4 PY)

This month gives you an opportunity to pay attention to loved ones and home or community duties and responsibilities. Enjoy social times with family and friends. This is your domestic month. Don't travel unless you're going to visit family.

Be sure to maintain peaceful relationships, make domestic improvements, and be emotionally responsive. Help to create and maintain a harmonious environment in your home. The time is right to settle down, deepen love, and create harmony. You can enjoy sharing chores and good times with family or friends. Take time to enjoy children and to participate in children's activities.

This is a good time to enjoy the pleasures of romance, love, and marriage. Try to keep your emotions in balance. You may have to work through and solve domestic difficulties or problems in your personal relationship. It will be important for you to show a great deal of affection. In fact, the more love you give, the more you will receive. Be mature, devoted, and trustworthy when dealing with emotions. Don't be stubborn, intolerant, or worrying. Remind yourself that worry is payment for something that hasn't happened.

At times, situations will arise that require you to sacrifice some of your personal desires. Patience, consideration of others' feelings, and caring attitudes will help resolve problems. Use this month to be of service to those you care about. Give of yourself taking time to teach, pacify, and indicate approval. Through serving others you may find doors opening to new opportunities. Continue to exercise patience in regard to your projects as some ventures still need time to grow.

Use your imagination and express yourself artistically. Write, paint, cook, sing, or play a musical instrument. The focus on this month is to provide a peaceful, happy, and beautiful environment in your home.

## March Vibrations (4 PY)

This month gives you an opportunity to spend time alone, to analyze and clarify your goals, to learn from the past, and to plan for the future. Give yourself time to evaluate your present situation. Think about ventures that interest you. Try to study the possibilities, learning all you can to get a good understanding of the potential of some of the ventures you may be interested in. You may enlist the aid of professionals (lawyers, therapists, doctors, counselors) or look into religious or metaphysical studies. You'll seem to be drawn to the unusual and you may learn something of significance for the future.

Instead of taking action this month, wait and analyze current legal dealings, questionable relationships, and future plans or goals. You should have a broad-minded, analytical, and critical point of view. But watch that you don't become too intellectual, thinking only from your mind, remember to use your heart, too.

You will probably have to discuss your need to spend time by yourself with close friends and family members so that they don't feel neglected. Quarrelling or creating arguments to gain time alone isn't advisable. Instead, be honest with others and let them know you just need some time to think about things by yourself.

This isn't the month to be aggressive, sociable, or to pursue commercial ambitions. Think before speaking and examine the opinions of others carefully. Don't take what others say as gospel unless you are sure. Be a little secretive; don't reveal your thoughts.

Take time to be alone, read, study, research, write, teach, or enjoy philosophical conversations. Wait for the telephone to ring instead of being the one to call. This month you must be patient, tolerant, and willing to spend time alone. If possible, spend some time in the country or change your diet and exercise. Go for long walks. Take breaks to maintain a good spirit. Take care of your health. This is a good month to schedule a checkup with a doctor or dentist.

## April Vibrations (4 PY)

This month gives you an opportunity to take control of business and financial matters. You should rely on yourself, be forceful, self-confident, and act decisively. You will gain much if you approach matters in a businesslike manner, dress with dignity, and express yourself with authority. You will have more ability to make things happen with regard to business or financial matters than in any other month. You'll begin to see movement in some of your ventures. This isn't the time for vacations or undisciplined behavior.

Money could be an issue, and you'll have to make a major decision involving finances. It will be important for you not to procrastinate. Opportunities for advancement, recognition, financial improvement, and business expansion are there, but only happen if you are organized, tactful, and persuasive. Use a concentrated effort to get your projects underway. Exercise caution in all matters of trade, especially when buying or selling property, goods and services. Contracts, agreements, and negotiations will tax your resources, but remain focused and in control of your feelings. Avoiding quarrels or misunderstandings will be difficult, but try to remain calm in spite of the problems. Continue to use patience and faith as you wait for things to progress.

Associate with high-powered and enterprising people to help you take advantage of the opportunities. If you advertise and promote the projects you started eight or nine months ago, exceptional results will be achieved. Hard work and long hours may strain personal relationships.

## May Vibrations (4 PY)

This month gives you an opportunity to complete projects, be charitable, tolerant, and compassionate. You're getting ready to move on to a new activity. Use this time to help others, be generous, kind, and inspire or counsel those who are in need of your support. Try to give of yourself with little thought of reward. At times, situations will arise requiring you to have an unselfish, broad-minded attitude. Give blood, visit the elderly, needy, or sick and take a book, a treat, or a listening ear.

The projects, activities, or relationships that began eight or nine months ago are either completed or abandoned, causing you to readjust to different circumstances. Even though you may have seen the ending coming, relationships with friends or coworkers will likely be connected to much drama and strong emotions. Other endings will surprise you. Try to be understanding and compassionate regardless of the situation.

A new romantic possibility will present itself, but this isn't the time to begin anything new. Forcing your will on others will backfire. Eventually you will come to realize that endings are necessary in order to open doors to new interests and possibilities you've been thinking about. As the month ends you'll find yourself looking forward to exciting prospects in the future.

Take a long-distance trip if it's within your budget. This month can be used to meet with notable or helpful people who have the contacts or abilities to help further your ambitions. Your reputation may be enhanced by group interactions, auditions, and public appearances. Express yourself artistically, using your imagination, intuition, and inspiration for artistic creation. Write, paint, play a musical instrument, sing, or experiment with a new recipe.

## June Vibrations (4 PY)

This month will be active, full of new people, situations, and ideas. It seems as though things are finally falling into place. This is definitely a time to start a new activity, friendship, or vocation. A change may come into effect, bringing new solutions to some old problems, take the initiative to move yourself forward. You'll be put in the driver's seat. It's up to you to act responsibly and to take care of all of the work that's involved.

This month things get accomplished that were on the brink of completion three months ago but didn't materialize. Even though there will be a lot of work to do, you'll look forward to creating something tangible for your future. Be aggressive and make changes. Break up old conditions you don't like and strengthen weak areas. Base your decisions on independent and intellectual evaluations because you probably won't get any help or encouragement from others. In fact, this is a time for you to assert your independence and individuality. You may see yourself differently as you begin to act with more confidence and determination.

Take a chance if the odds are in your favor. Be yourself and emphasize your abilities. Use originality and creativity, but don't go overboard and irritate or alienate others. Take time to meet with friends and family so they don't feel left out. You might have to explain your personal goals to those close to you so they understand what's going on in your head.

## July Vibrations (4 PY)

Although this will be a busy month, there will be an opportunity for you to interact with friends and lovers and to make others happy. You feel the urge to act, but this isn't the time to be ambitious or to make any material changes. Instead, this is a time for you to work patiently, taking care of the details that may slow you down later. If you go after something or try to make things happen quicker, you will probably end up sabotaging the project, and your efforts will be wasted. Temporary delays will cause feelings of limitation and restriction. It's best for you to have faith and wait patiently for developments, even though it may seem as though nothing is happening.

Rest and allow friends, lovers, and business associates time to think and adjust to things that may differ from their personal desires. At times, situations arise that require you to be diplomatic, considerate, and tactful. Don't force issues. You may have to compromise and do the little things that you overlooked last month. You may be called upon to lend a helping hand to friends or family members, or assist them in their ventures. Use this month to cooperate with others while quietly working on your own projects.

Be open-minded as you listen to others' sly remarks or constructive criticisms that may prove to be helpful. You may be overly sensitive and self-conscious, taking what others say the "wrong way" and end up with hurt feelings. Don't be that way. Instead, spend some quality time with a loved one and try to be adaptable, understanding, and courteous while you wait for developments.

## August Vibrations (4 PY)

This month you will have an opportunity to feel happy, cheerful, playful, and self-expressive. The year has been difficult, with lots of hard work and little room for fun. Now is the time to enjoy friends, to entertain and be entertained. There will be may parties or social functions to attend, and energetic people to meet. Situations will arise requiring you to have an attractive appearance and to put on a happy face. This is a good month to take a short vacation or to travel, as long as you can afford to take time off. Actually, a change of pace might do you a world of good.

Although you'll have a lively social life, it will be important for you to remain constructive and not shirk your responsibilities. You'll still have to take care of the duties (business or domestic) that need to be done to keep things running smoothly. Exercise caution so that you don't scatter your energies or go off in all sorts of different directions.

Call old friends you haven't talked to in awhile; take a phone number at a party and make a new contact. The friends you meet may open doors to new opportunities, adding insight or creative thoughts to your endeavors.

Money doesn't seem to be such a problem this month. Shop for new clothes or decorate your home, but expect to lose money through frivolousness and extravagance. It's best to leave your credit card at home. Remember to use logic and practicality when looking to purchase things. Ask yourself if you really need an item before you buy it.

The projects you began four months ago will start to bloom. Use this month to talk about your ideas, show off your talents, and have fun with friends, lovers, and coworkers. All forms of communication will be important. Express yourself, use imagination, intuition, and inspiration in creative activities. Write, dance, paint, cook, or play a musical instrument. Just be creative and have fun!

*September Vibrations (4 PY)*

This month, through hard work, you'll have an opportunity to produce substantial results and build for the future. You must seriously apply yourself with regard to money, routines, and physical fitness. This month isn't the time to be lazy, disorganized, or impractical. Instead, you must use this month to reconstruct plans or projects and take care of any mistakes in finance or judgment. Put everything in order to get ventures under way. Situations will arise that demand a straightforward approach. Research your ideas and don't gamble on the unknown.

At times, you'll feel very limited and restricted. It's important that you take time to analyze the limitations or restrictions and see whether they are of your own making. If so, plan to eliminate them. You might have to change your point of view. An "attitude adjustment" could be in store and you might have to look at things from a different perspective. Realize that some limitations are unchangeable and you'll have to learn how to deal with them in a more satisfactory manner.

Watch that you don't over schedule yourself, causing yourself more stress. Tackle the work and try to keep your spirits high in spite of all you have to do. You might have to ask family members for their help in completing some tasks before the pressures mount and you blow up in frustration. This is a time to throw silly notions out the window and be practical.

You might have to take on more domestic responsibility. Work instead of talking about what needs to be done. Be efficient and stabilize your finances. Create a budget and stick to it. Follow through on commitments, organize time, and above all don't waste your energy. During these stressful times take a few moments to rest and relax; taking short breaks will ease the tensions. Stress can bring on health problems, so take care of your health when ailments bother you.

*October Vibrations (4 PY)*

This month offers you an opportunity to expand your horizons, to progress, and make changes. You should get out and meet new people, see new places, experience new activities, and have unusual opportunities. You'll have plenty of chances to enjoy people and participate in social activities. If romance is what you're looking for, this month offers new and interesting possibilities for love relationships. Take a chance on luck and love, although love affairs may not last very long.

Unusual ideas, travel, and a drive toward less responsibility are in the air. In fact, if you travel, you may find strange or unexpected possibilities. Get away and take a break from the hustle and bustle of the past months if you can, but remain mindful that you still have to take care of your obligations. Delegating some of the work will allow you more freedom to socialize. Try to minimize responsibilities if you can, but don't ignore them.

Watch legal commitments and expect conflicts and outbursts. If you decide to pursue a new venture, be careful and make sure that it's got potential for expansion and growth. Some opportunities that are presented may fade quickly. The trick to getting the most out of this month is to look for something tangible. Situations will arise requiring you to follow a hunch. If the odds are in your favor, take a chance. Drop the old and grab onto the new only if there is a possibility for long-term benefits. Be venturesome. Try something different, spontaneous, dress to attract attention, and begin an exercise regimen.

This month, be careful not to run yourself ragged, putting too many irons into the fire. Don't lack focus, becoming unreliable, temperamental, and frustrated. Unexpected possibilities are around every corner, so be flexible, broad-minded, and full of energy.

## November Vibrations (4 PY)

This month gives you an opportunity to pay attention to the loved ones you haven't had much time to visit with during the year. Home or community duties and responsibilities will need to be taken care of. This is your domestic month, a time to be available to others with a helping hand. Don't travel unless you're going to visit family. Be sure to maintain peaceful relationships, make domestic improvements, and be emotionally responsive. The time is right to settle down, deepen love, and create harmony. You can enjoy sharing chores and good times with family or friends. Take time to enjoy children and to participate in children's activities. This is a good time to enjoy the pleasures of romance, love, and marriage. Keep your emotions in balance and show a great deal of affection. In fact, the more love you give, the more you will receive.

At times, situations will arise that require you to sacrifice some of your personal desires. Use this month to be of service to a family member who is having health problems and needs some special attention. Give of yourself when necessary and without resentment. Take time to teach, pacify, and indicate approval. Through serving others you may find doors opening to new opportunities.

Be mature, devoted, and trustworthy when dealing with emotions. Don't be stubborn, intolerant, or worrying. There may be some legal or financial matters for you to deal with that came as a consequence of your earlier actions.

Use your imagination and express yourself artistically. Write, paint, cook, sing, or play a musical instrument. The focus on this month is to provide a peaceful, happy, and beautiful environment in your home.

## December Vibrations (4 PY)

The holiday season is upon you and it seems you don't feel much like partying. This month gives you an opportunity to spend time alone, to analyze and clarify your goals, to learn from the past, and to plan for the future. Your thoughts might wander back to the last couple of years as you evaluate your progress. What have you managed to accomplish? What are your goals for next year? It might be a good idea for you to think about what you want to do during the next few years, and give some thought to planning.

During the month you may enlist the aid of professionals (lawyers, doctors, therapists, counselors) or look into religious or metaphysical studies. You'll seem to be drawn to the unusual.

Instead of taking action this month, wait and analyze current legal dealings, questionable relationships, and future plans or goals. You should have a broad-minded, analytical, and critical point of view. Watch that you don't become too intellectual, thinking only from your mind, remember to use your heart, too.

Chances are you may learn something of significance for the future. This isn't the month to be aggressive, sociable, or to pursue commercial ambitions. There will still be work that needs to be done, but you'll start to notice a difference in the work load. Think before speaking and examine the opinions of others carefully. Don't take what others say as gospel unless you are sure. Be a little secretive; don't reveal your thoughts. Take time to be alone, read, study, research, write, teach, or enjoy philosophical conversations.

Wait for the telephone to ring instead of being the one to call. This month you must be patient, tolerant, and willing to spend time alone. If possible, spend some time in the country or change your diet and exercise. Go for long walks. Take care of any health matters that present themselves. Get yourself into shape for the excitement and activity that's coming your way next year.

# 5 PERSONAL YEAR VIBRATION

This will be a year for change, growth, fun, and freedom. An important change in residence, work, or family situation is likely and may not be due to your initiative. You must take advantage of the change and use it to help you move forward. Your challenge during the year will be to remain focused on long-term goals, making an effort to sort out important projects and see them through from start to finish.

After the work, diligence and down-to-earth conditions of last year, the change and freedom from routine should be very agreeable to you. At times you may feel unsettled, but on the whole the year offers an opportunity for advancement and progress. You will find life brings you many opportunities. It will be difficult for you to stay focused and not waste energy or go off in every direction.

Money could be a problem, here today, not so much tomorrow, but there when you need it if you are willing to work and not resist routines.

If you try to keep up-to-date and have an open mind, you'll be able to refresh your life, clearing up old conditions for more personal freedom and advancement. Take a chance on unknowns and don't be afraid of making spontaneous decisions, as long as you remain constructive.

Experiment with fashions and fads, foods or hobbies. Fresh thoughts enter your mind and you'll benefit from reading new philosophies and studying different subjects. You'll be attracted to the mysterious and to psychic phenomena. If you have a talent in writing, public speaking, or the arts, you'll find life offers opportunities for you to enhance your abilities. The lines of work that require the support of the people will find success.

This year offers a chance to be a bit self-indulgent, informal, and sociable. You'll find many people will be attracted to you through your charm and charisma. It seems as though suddenly you have a magical ability to promote yourself and your talents. Since your personal magnetism and sex appeal are at their peak, exercise caution in all sexual matters. Pregnancy or sexually transmitted diseases can happen if you're not careful.

Without change you cannot grow, but that does not mean that you should scatter your energy by being restless or impulsive. Instead, it means to plan a definite goal for advancement and to be intelligent when making the adjustments and decisions necessary for improvement.

You should watch feelings of restlessness, frustration, impatience, or resentment towards those who hold you down or bind you. Haste makes waste and could lead to deep regret later on in life. Nothing can be gained through quarreling or through burning your bridges behind you. Letting your restless feelings get out of hand can lead to carelessness, sloppy behavior, or illegal dealings. Legal activities need to be taken care of with good counsel; you could be involved in legal settlements, most likely in your favor.

If you feel that you can progress only by breaking up old conditions, you must be sure to do this in a constructive way. Don't jump impulsively from the frying pan into the fire. To get the best out of this year, all changes should be to the advantage of others as well as yourself. Use wisdom and discretion to break up some of the old routine and turn the details over to others.

Strive to live in harmony with others. The eventfulness, excitable conditions, and your own inner unrest, will make this year very active and tricky. Even though they may confuse you, accept the changes, new contacts, and new opportunities in the spirit of progress and advancement. Be flexible and follow your curiosity. Get fun out of meeting new opportunities and conditions. Be versatile in your thoughts and resourceful in your actions. Plan or you'll have regrets later as you'll experience problems due to haste or impatience.

Do something new to freshen up your home, social and business activities. Your business may require you to travel or to be away from home. The road will be bumpy with many ups and downs regarding your finances, relationships, and business. Hang in there, remain focused, and keep your eyes on future benefits.

Along with the good times, the increase of activity and experience brings trials and temptations. Watch the tendency to overindulge in the sexual and sensual, eating and drinking. Escapism through indulgences will be tempting and you will be less willing to follow the rules this year.

You'll benefit by trying to control your erratic and totally unpredictable behavior. In fact, keeping yourself disciplined this year could be a difficult task. Legal troubles could result if you are not careful. Think twice and consider the consequences before you indulge in self-destructive behaviors. Self-discipline will be absolutely necessary if you want to succeed.

During the year you will be tested in your ability to feel free and easy yet remain constructive. If the timing is right, your chance to move ahead is excellent, although rewards may not be as great as you expect. This year has a few strokes of good luck for the person who is ready to make room for unusual methods, ideas, and attitudes.

Expect the world to send you surprises, especially in May and September. You'll find your mailbox filled with credit card applications or opportunities to become involved in get-rich-quick schemes. Use good judgment and think before leaping. Watch what you sign and think twice about making long-term or long-range agreements. If you don't think things through, you may have to make changes or adjustments later.

Progress will depend on showing tolerance and profiting from new experiences, and not anticipating the end result or assuming how people will interact. Your attitude is very important; it's best to go with the flow. Social activities will lead to contacts with impulsive, freewheeling, energetic people who will point the way to new directions. Don't be modest. Instead, try to promote and publicize yourself and your projects. Open your mind to new possibilities. Perhaps it's time to turn a hobby into a money-making enterprise. Others will be attracted by your energy and enthusiasm if you make the effort to get out, travel, meet people and shake hands.

If married, expect a rekindling of the focus on love and passion. Work on any underlying friction in your family relationships. If there's tension in your home, try to remain balanced and calm and remember to think before speaking. Quarreling only causes problems and can lead to separations or legal troubles. Always think before speaking, considering the other person's feelings as well as your own. Kind words work wonders. If you take a real interest in your spouse's work or career, you'll find yourselves growing closer together.

If single, expect to meet exiting, passionate, provocative and extraordinary strangers. If a lover or friend remains in the picture through April of next year, they are potential marriage partners.

If you flow with the tide of the year and refrain from acting on impulse alone, this year should end up on a positive and successful note.

### Personal Month Vibrations in a 5 Personal Year

The following is a brief outline of the vibrations you can expect during the 5 Personal Year (for a more detailed description of what a specific month has in store for you, read the information found under the month heading, at the end of this section).

In January there is likely to be a change or expansion in your domestic situation which will create new excitement and adventure. You could meet your future mate, or a new friend, find a new job direction, or turn a hobby into a vocation.

February brings a time for you to maintain peace of mind and think things out quietly. You may be unemployed, but don't worry, money will come in when you need it most. You will feel a strain between what you want and what you have, leaving you feeling limited and restricted. Find time to be alone when you feel frustration building. Keep demands to a minimum and try to compromise.

In March, if you're looking for a job, you might get something better than you expected. Exercise self-control and use good judgment. Take risks on what you know or on what you have researched well. The year starts out with a restless urge for change and times could be tense through April. You may feel trapped or bound in your job, marriage or personal relationship. It's always difficult to decide when it's best to leave or to make significant changes.

April brings conclusions, an opportunity to forgive, and a decision about new things. An important experience or relationship may breakdown or end, allowing you to pursue a different, more progressive course. You may have to yield control. Don't force matters. Avoid personal demands based on hasty action, impulsiveness, or words spoken in anger.

May brings time for vacations, sensual pleasures and change. This will be a competitive month in business, with excellent prospects for growth. Very exciting possibilities emerge, although they may need to be tested for longevity. Design, travel, explore or take a chance if the odds are in your favor. Be yourself and emphasize your abilities.

June shows strong romantic possibilities and a temporary delay in money, but don't worry, it will come when you need it most. This is a time for cooperation and changes in friendships. Small details will make a big difference.

The summer will be an exciting and adventurous time in your life. Doors can open now. Try not be too impatient, be careful of what you say, but push ahead. Over-confidence can create needless errors when making decisions. Stay focused and express yourself in unusual and unique ways.

August brings changes in work schedules and practical problems to think about for future actions. You may feel restricted and uncomfortable. Make a list of goals and put everything in order if you want to succeed.

September should show thrilling change or freedom. Don't make any major decisions in this unstable time. Be careful of feelings of resentment and try not to get into conflicts, though they may be needed to clear the air. Expect some sexual problems. Self-pity gains very little. Let go of the past and concentrate on the future. You may travel or start a part-time job.

October is a good time to feel happy and secure, and to enjoy the deep pleasures of romance. Are you getting engaged or married?

November gives you a chance to slow down and think about the year's experiences. Don't have an affair, especially with a married person. A self-contained or inflexible attitude may cause problems in communication and interfere with opportunities. Don't be stubborn.

Financial problems may have you worried, but money will come in its own time. By the end of the year you'll experience excellent business opportunities and long-awaited change. Work hard and reap success.

## January Vibrations (5 PY)

The new year begins with an opportunity for you to pay attention to loved ones and home or community duties and responsibilities. This is your domestic month. Don't travel unless you're going to visit family. Be sure to maintain peaceful relationships, make domestic improvements, and be emotionally responsive.

The time is right to settle down, deepen love, and create harmony. You can enjoy sharing chores and good times with family or friends. Take time to enjoy children and to participate in children's activities. Keep your emotions in balance and show a great deal of affection. In fact, the more love you give, the more you will receive. This is a good time to enjoy the pleasures of romance, love, and marriage.

At times, situations will arise that require you to sacrifice some of your personal desires. There may be left-over duties from last month that will have to be taken care of now. Don't neglect your chores, even though the chores get in the way of other activities you'd rather pursue.

Use this month to be of service, to teach, pacify, and indicate approval. Through serving others you may find doors opening to new opportunities. There is the indication of change or improvement in your home life, which will allow more freedom for you and others. Think before making significant changes.

Be mature, devoted, and trustworthy when dealing with your emotions. Keeping feelings under control may not be easy at this time, but try your best. You may be called to help others do the same. Don't be stubborn, intolerant, or worrying. Worry is a form of payment for something that doesn't exist right now. Don't fret over things you can't control. Have faith that things will work out.

Use your imagination and express yourself artistically. Take time to write, paint, cook, or play a musical instrument. The focus on this month is to provide a peaceful, happy, and beautiful environment in your home.

## February Vibrations (5 PY)

This month gives you an opportunity to spend time alone, to analyze and clarify your goals, to learn from the past, and to plan for the future. You may have to enlist the aid of professionals (lawyers, doctors, therapists, counselors, agents). You'll seem to be drawn to the unusual and may want to take time to look into religious or metaphysical studies. Meditation can help you decide what you need to do.

Instead of taking action this month, wait and analyze current legal dealings, questionable relationships, and future plans or goals. Restlessness will cause problems. Acting impulsively may make it difficult for you to obtain the goals you've been working to achieve. You should have a broad-minded, analytical, and critical point of view. But watch that you don't become too intellectual, thinking only from your mind. It will be important for you to remember to use your heart too.

This isn't the month to be aggressive, sociable, or to pursue commercial ambitions. Think before speaking and examine others opinions carefully. Try to avoid quarrels and misunderstandings. Don't take what others say as gospel unless you are sure. Be a little secretive and don't reveal your thoughts. Take time to be alone, read, study, research, write, teach, or enjoy philosophical conversations.

Wait for the telephone to ring instead of being the one to call. This month you must be patient, tolerant, and willing to spend time alone. If possible, spend some time in the country or change your diet and exercise. Go for long walks in nature. Listen to the small still voice inside and you may learn something of significance for the future.

Take care of your health. Make sure to discuss any problems or concerns with your doctor. Don't procrastinate when it comes to health matters.

## March Vibrations (5 PY)

This month gives you an opportunity to take control of business and financial matters. You should rely on yourself, be forceful, self-confident, act decisively, approach matters in a businesslike manner, dress with dignity, and express yourself with authority. You will have more ability to make things happen with regard to business or financial matters than in any other month. If new business or financial ventures appear, check them out for longevity. Perhaps you'll be offered a new situation in an entirely different direction, which will end up bringing you more freedom in the long run.

You'll have to make a major decision involving money. Don't procrastinate.

Make up your mind so that you can take full advantage of the opportunities presented. Carefully study the situations and possibilities for advancement that present themselves. Don't underestimate the amount of work required to get ventures off the ground. Opportunities for advancement, recognition, financial improvement, and business expansion are there, but only happen if you are organized, tactful, and persuasive.

Be open to meeting new types of people, friends, and business associates. Associate with high-powered and enterprising people to help you take advantage of the opportunities. If you advertise and promote the projects you started eight or nine months ago, exceptional results will be achieved.

Hard work and long hours may strain personal relationships. This isn't the time for vacations or undisciplined behavior.

## April Vibrations (5 PY)

This month gives you an opportunity to complete projects, be charitable, tolerant, and compassionate. Use this month to help others, to be generous, kind, and inspire or counsel those who are in need of your support. You should try to give of yourself with little thought of reward. At times, situations will arise requiring you to have an unselfish, broad-minded attitude. Give blood, visit the elderly, needy, or sick and take a book, a treat, or a listening ear.

The projects, activities, or relationships that began eight or nine months ago are either completed or abandoned, causing you to readjust to different circumstances. You may be surprised at the termination of a floundering relationship. This ending may not be desired by you; however, it will allow you a great deal of personal freedom which will become more apparent as the year moves forward. The endings will likely be connected to much drama and strong emotions. Keep your cool and try to be understanding and compassionate, regardless of the situation. Be understanding and compassionate with your own feelings as well.

This isn't the time to begin anything new or to force your will on others. Take a long-distance trip if it's within your budget. This month can be used to meet with notable or helpful people who have the contacts or abilities to help further your ambitions. Your reputation may be enhanced by group interactions, auditions, and public appearances.

Express yourself artistically, using your imagination, intuition, and inspiration for artistic creation. Write, paint, play a musical instrument, or learn to cook a new dish.

# 5 PERSONAL YEAR VIBRATION

## May Vibrations (5 PY)

This month will be active, and you should take the initiative. A change may come into effect, bringing new solutions to some old problems. You'll be put in the driver's seat and it's up to you to act.

This month things get accomplished that were on the brink of completion three months ago but didn't materialize. May will be full of new people, situations, and ideas. Be aggressive and make changes. Break up old conditions you don't like and strengthen weak areas. Base your decisions on independent and intellectual evaluations because you probably won't get any help or encouragement from others. It's best for you to do things your own way and not worry about what others may say or think, especially if their views differ from yours.
What others think of you is really none of your business. Take a chance if the odds are in your favor, but be careful not to act impulsively.

This is a month for beginnings: start a new activity, friendship, or vocation. Be yourself and emphasize your abilities. Travel if you can. You may begin to see yourself differently. Use originality and creativity, but don't go overboard and irritate or alienate others.

## June Vibrations (5 PY)

This month offers an opportunity for you to interact with friends and lovers and to make others happy. Although you feel the urge to act, this isn't the time to be ambitious or to make any material changes. Instead, this is a time for you to work quietly, to take care of the details that may slow you down later.

Wait patiently for developments, even though it may seem as though nothing is happening. Rest and allow friends, lovers, and business associates time to think and adjust to things that may differ from their personal desires. Misunderstandings and frayed nerves could be difficult to handle. At times, situations arise that require you to be diplomatic, considerate, and tactful. Don't force issues. You may have to compromise and do the little things that you overlooked last month. Use this month to cooperate with others while working on your projects, or help others with their ventures. You'll find those you help will be appreciative of your support.

Be open-minded as you listen to others sly remarks or constructive criticisms that may prove to be helpful. You may be overly sensitive and self-conscious, taking what others say the "wrong way" and end up with hurt feelings. Don't be that way. Try to be adaptable, understanding, and courteous while you wait for developments. Your sensitivity could lead you to some profound spiritual insights which will open doors to new directions.

## July Vibrations (5 PY)

This month you will have an opportunity to feel happy, cheerful, playful, and self-expressive. This is a month to enjoy friends, to entertain and be entertained. You'll have an unusual, active social life. You'll be invited to spend time with friends and acquaintances, attending parties, and meeting new energetic people. Situations will arise requiring you to have an attractive appearance and to put on a happy face. Call old friends you haven't talked to in awhile; take a phone number at a party and make a new contact. The friends you meet may open doors to new opportunities.

Allow time for special, quality activities with your children. Enjoy your family. Express yourself, using your imagination, intuition, and inspiration in creative activities. Write, dance, paint, cook, or play a musical instrument. Take time out to be creative and have fun!

This is a good month to take a short vacation or to travel. Trips will bring a sense of adventure and add exciting stimulation to your life. Shop for new clothes or decorate your home, but expect to lose money through frivolousness and extravagance. This month it's best to leave your credit card at home.

The projects you began four months ago will start to bloom. There will be work to be done, but remember to leave some time for fun and relaxation. Use this month to talk about your ideas, show off your talents, and have fun with friends, lovers, and coworkers. All forms of communication will be important.

## August Vibrations (5 PY)

This month, through hard work, you'll have an opportunity to produce substantial results and build for the future. You must seriously apply yourself with regard to money, routines, and physical fitness. This month isn't the time to be lazy, disorganized, or impractical. Instead, you must use this month to reconstruct plans or projects and take care of any mistakes in finance or judgment. Put everything in order to get ventures under way. You might have to change some plans you made last month in order to get the work done.

Situations will arise that demand a straightforward approach. Research your ideas and don't gamble on the unknown. At times, you'll probably feel limited or restricted. It's important that you take time to analyze the limitations or restrictions and see whether they are of your own making. If so, plan to eliminate them. You might have to change your point of view. Perhaps an "attitude adjustment" could be in store. Some limitations are unchangeable and you'll have to learn how to deal with them in a more satisfactory manner.

You might have to take on more domestic responsibility. Work instead of talking about what needs to be done. You probably won't feel like taking care of your domestic responsibilities, but if you don't you'll regret it later. Get things out of the way that could hold you down at a later date. You may feel irritated. Keep these feelings under control. Be patient when dealing with others, as disagreements or upsets will cause problems. Try to remain patient and handle others with kindness and consideration.

Be efficient and stabilize your finances. Follow through on commitments, organize time, and above all don't waste your energy. You may feel a bit stressed, so remember to take care of your health. This is a time to throw silly notions out the window and be practical.

## September Vibrations (5 PY)

This month offers you an opportunity to expand your horizons, to progress, and make changes. You should get out and meet new people, see new places, experience new activities, and have unusual opportunities. Whimsical ideas, travel, and a drive toward less responsibility are in the air. In fact, if you travel, you may find unusual or unexpected possibilities.

Try to minimize responsibilities if you can, but don't ignore them. Watch legal commitments and expect conflicts and outbursts. Take a chance on luck and love, although love affairs may not last. Situations will arise requiring you to follow a hunch. If the odds are in your favor, take a chance. Be venturesome. Try something different, spontaneous, dress to attract attention, and exercise. Drop the old and look for the new. Be careful not to run yourself ragged.

It's important that you don't lack focus, becoming unreliable, temperamental, and frustrated. If you feel a restless need for physical stimulation, curb your tendencies or you'll find yourself getting in your own way. Unproductive behavior won't benefit you.

Unexpected possibilities are around every corner, so be flexible, broad-minded, and full of energy. Travel if you can, get out and smell the flowers, initiate some changes. Have fun!

## October Vibrations (5 PY)

This month gives you an opportunity to pay attention to loved ones and home or community duties and responsibilities. You can have fun with family members and close friends. Be sure to maintain peaceful relationships, make domestic improvements, and be emotionally responsive. The time is right to settle down, deepen love, and create harmony.

This is your domestic month. You can enjoy sharing chores and good times with family or friends. Domestic duties may get in the way of your plans with family members and those you hold dear to your heart. Feeling frustrated and irritated with the chores won't do you any good. Do the work you have to do and then go play with your family.

Take time to enjoy children and to participate in children's activities. Keep your emotions in balance and show a great deal of affection. In fact, the more love you give, the more you will receive. This is a good time to enjoy the pleasures of romance, love, and marriage. At times, situations will arise that require you to sacrifice some of your personal desires.

Use this month to be of service, to teach, pacify, and indicate approval. Through serving others you may find doors opening to new opportunities. Be mature, devoted, and trustworthy when dealing with emotions. Don't be stubborn, intolerant, or worrying. Use your imagination and express yourself artistically. The focus on this month is to provide a peaceful, happy, and beautiful environment in your home. Don't travel unless you're going to visit family.

## November Vibrations (5 PY)

This month gives you an opportunity to spend time alone, to reflect on your life, analyze and clarify your goals, to learn from the past, and to plan for the future. You may enlist the aid of professionals (lawyers, doctors, therapists, counselors), or look into religious or metaphysical studies. You'll be drawn to the unusual.

Instead of taking action this month, wait and analyze current legal dealings, questionable relationships, and future plans or goals. Approach your life with a broad-minded, analytical, and critical point of view. Don't become too intellectual, thinking only from your mind, remember to use your heart, too.

This isn't the month to be aggressive, sociable, or to pursue commercial ambitions. Think before speaking and examine others opinions carefully. Don't take what others say as gospel unless you are sure. Be a little secretive, it's best not to reveal your thoughts. Take time to be alone, read, study, research, write, teach, or enjoy philosophical conversations.

Make sure your loved ones know this is a time for you to spend time alone, quietly contemplating all that's happened during the year. They may feel alienated or neglected. It's best to let them know what's going on with you so they can understand.

Wait for the telephone to ring instead of being the one to call. This month you must be patient, tolerant, and willing to spend time alone. If possible, spend some time in the country or change your diet and exercise. Get out in nature and go for long walks or hike a new trail. You may learn something of significance for the future if you listen to your inner voice. Take care of your health.

## December Vibrations (5 PY)

This month gives you another opportunity to take control of business and financial matters. You should rely on yourself, be forceful, self-confident, act decisively, approach matters in a businesslike manner, dress with dignity, and express yourself with authority.

You'll have to make a major decision involving money. Don't procrastinate. Think about your options and go with what you feel is best. Opportunities for advancement, recognition, financial improvement, and business expansion are there, but only happen if you are organized, tactful, and persuasive.

Associate with high-powered and enterprising people to help you take advantage of new opportunities. If you advertise and promote the projects you started eight or nine months ago, exceptional results will be achieved. Hard work and long hours may strain personal relationships. This isn't the time for vacations or undisciplined behavior; however, there will be special times for friends and family during the festive holiday season.

# 6 PERSONAL YEAR VIBRATION

The 6 Personal Year is called the year of love, marriage, and sacrifice. Life will bring you events and opportunities emphasizing responsibility and domestic affairs. Service is the key to your success and happiness. This year, the focus is on home, family, marriage, responsibility, service and sacrifice. There will be obligations to pay up, responsibilities to meet and duty to accept. If your motives include truth, justice, charity, unselfishness and humanity in everything you do, you are likely to have a very satisfying year.

Creating a harmonious atmosphere will be very important, for love, money, health, and friendship can suddenly depart if disharmony persists. Make a special effort to resolve tensions between you and your loved ones, for love can come to you if you are generous, loving and unselfish enough to receive it. Don't act childish, shirk work, or make impulsive changes. There will be a lot of emotion in the air, causing tensions between loved ones.

This year, look at your life and realize how much you truly love your mate, or how little love you have in your life. Problems will arise if dominance or self-centeredness is present, or if standards are broken and selfish interests are followed. Control issues, either yours or your mate's, will backfire. Your union may crumble if love isn't true, or if the love you have is betrayed. This year, the whole love issue comes to the forefront, its joys and its problems.

If you travel, expect to find problems waiting to be solved at home. Social activities, creative endeavors, and trips should center around your home and family. You'll find friends and family come to you for inspiration, guidance, or a shoulder to cry on. You will learn the meaning of the old saying, "What goes around comes around," for through expressing sympathy, understanding, and love you can even gain financially during the year.

This year, talk matters over with family and friends, understand and consider everyone's needs, and try to be as giving and unselfish as possible. Harder said than done at times. Others will impose upon you or try to take advantage of your good nature; neighbors, friends and relatives come over or call for help; you may have to take care of the sick or elderly; your job seems bogged down; children have more illnesses, problems, and arguments that need your attention. Bills get out of hand, unexpected repairs arise, and your mate seems uncooperative. If you accept these situations as a privilege instead of a burden, money will come to meet the obligations. Learning to accept duties with a cheerful and willing attitude will be difficult; however, you'll be rewarded for your sacrifices in the long run.

You will accomplish most by putting others first and resolving the immediate crisis. It's an easy time for false martyrdom. At times you may think: Oh, look at all I've done for others with no appreciation! Face the demands. Forget the drama.

Don't object to staying home, devoting time to listen, helping someone else, or supporting a loved one's desires. Serve unselfishly, but be careful not to let others take advantage of your desire to be of assistance. Guard yourself against being a doormat, but understand the occasional need for sacrifice.

Don't be discouraged, this year isn't totally filled with drudgery. Try to recognize this as a once-in-nine-year chance to be an understanding, loving, and conscientious team player and adviser. Change your attitude about your situation, find another viewpoint. Your unselfish efforts, along with the obligations you undertake this year, will be appreciated and provide experiences that make you wiser. Those who receive your assistance during this demanding time span will reciprocate by supporting your ambitions during the next three years.

If married, this is a year to make home improvements and share precious moments with family and friends. This is a good year to get married or to continue in marriage as long as emotions are balanced and feelings clearly and openly expressed. Hiding or disguising feelings will only cause more problems. Failure to communicate your feelings will lead to confusion and difficulties.

This year, the tensions in your marriage may be aggravated and, although you may be uncomfortable, now is the time to resolve the causes. If tensions are allowed to remain, the marriage could come to an end, either in separation or divorce. If problems are discussed with understanding and a consideration of everyone's wants and needs, the marriage could be reborn on a greater level of mutual love, respect, and cooperation. Both you and your spouse should look very closely at your childhood conflicts with parents. You'll be surprised to recognize little traits and irritating attitudes in yourselves, similar to those of your parents. Don't let your emotions get the best of you. Try to remain calm and talk things out if you can.

If single, this year can stimulate the desire for companionship, family, and marriage. Thinking about old times and old romances can make this a lonesome year. Moodiness and depression can get to you if you dwell too long without attempting to understand the cause Very possibly, a lover or friend who came into your life last year may be a candidate for a long-term relationship and you could begin to make plans for a permanent union. You may feel a strong desire to get settled, both in business and domestic affairs, and the end of the year should bring you a great deal of satisfaction in this respect.

This year, whether you marry a person or a job, commitments made must be given top priority. In business or domestic affairs, expect to be resourceful, determined, and to stand up for what you believe in. There may be a dominant, selfish, tactless, or possessive individual who causes you unhappiness or oppresses you either in business or at home. At times you will experience feelings of vulnerability, your emotions prone to turmoil. When dealing with authority figures, it's important for you to remain balanced and centered, and find the right emotional attitude toward others. You could have an opportunity to advance and improve your business or financial affairs.

New opportunities and achievements will bring added responsibility and a strain on your nerves. Don't "sweat the small stuff." You'll improve your health if you worry less about little things. Try to keep in mind that worry does you no good. This is a year for you to learn to release stress, to have faith in yourself and in what you're doing. Plan for the future, live each day as if it were your last, and don't fall asleep angry. You should make a personal resolution to settle differences at the end of each day and greet each morning free of hostility. The more love and affection given, the more returned.

Keep romantic notions and peaceful relationships foremost in your mind when you are called to make personal sacrifices for others. Be charitable and tolerant, a forgive and forget attitude will be best. To get the most this year has to offer, you must be satisfied, concerned with other people's problems, and demonstrate a great deal of love and affection. This year provides you with an opportunity to enjoy and experience what love is all about.

Many will turn to you for advice; you must be there to help, sometimes even to your own disadvantage. It will be best for you to learn to distinguish between helping and interfering. Offer advice only when asked and don't become upset if your advice isn't followed. Sometimes all people need is to talk to someone about what's bothering them.

At times you may find it necessary to take advice from friends, relatives, or those in authority. You should see improvement in all areas of your life if you are willing to make the adjustments and consider the good in others as well as in yourself. Keep your ideals high, and try to avoid any feeling of resentment because of unfairness. You can bring about the improvement and more settled conditions, which the year holds out to you, as long as you give out more generously than you receive. Live true to yourself this year and you may even have the opportunity to instill ideals into the hearts and minds of others.

It may seem this year offers little time to satisfy your own personal desires. Everyone else always comes first. Although this isn't a time for big accomplishments and things may seem to be at a standstill, know that endeavors outside the home are moving. Learn to accept the slow pace and demands on your time and money, and have faith that things are moving along even though you can't see where or how just yet.

Sometimes you may not be too clear about what you want out of life. During such times take a moment to contemplate and meditate. Life has a plan for you, waiting to be discovered and revealed. You may be intuitive, creative, and sensitive, feeling a strong artistic urge. Know that your inner self will guide you in the right direction.

### Personal Month Vibrations in a 6 Personal Year
The following is a brief outline of the vibrations you can expect during the 6 Personal Year (for a more detailed description of what a specific month has in store for you, read the information found under the month heading, at the end of this section).

The action of the year is slow and this may seem very noticeable during the first three months as you experience delays in your external affairs. Search your inner self, reconsider your motives and intent to find the keys to progress. Relationships and emotional ties may need to be examined at this time. It's best to take things as they come. This year you can't expect to be absorbed in personal desires or receive love without giving it.

At the beginning of the year your health could be a problem and you may need to rely on your family to take care of you. Worrying is unnecessary and can cause illness. Seek out the quiet of your mind, do some soul-searching.

February will be full of responsibility and hard work, you will have an opportunity to take control of business and financial matters. Unusual or exciting possibilities could conflict with family needs and desires and you may have to make a major decision regarding your domestic life.

March brings some conclusions and decisions. You may experience the loss of a job, relationship, relative or friend. Long-distance travel may involve inheritance or visiting a family member or service group. You'll feel a great deal of restriction and will need to make some emotional adjustments.

April brings new energy, vitality and a feeling of accomplishment. Buy a new house, start a new activity, friendship or vocation. You should see an increase in activity from April to August, with personal responsibilities and obligations coming to a peak through the fall and early winter months.

Use May to cooperate with others while working on your projects, or help others on their ventures. Be open-minded as you listen to others' sly remarks or constructive criticisms that may prove to be helpful. Rest and allow friends and lovers time to think and adjust to things that may differ from their personal desires.

June is a good month for a wedding, vacation or holiday. From June on, push your plans and adjustments forward. All forms of communication will be important.

July brings practical matters for you to manage by yourself. You will have an opportunity to organize your domestic life. Follow through on commitments, organize time, and above all don't waste your energy.

August is a good month to take that trip you've been thinking about this year. Conflicts on the home front may be unavoidable due to restlessness and a need for excessive physical stimulation. Don't eat or drink too much, avoid drugs, and watch sexual encounters. Too much of a good thing could cause problems; try to learn from past mistakes instead of repeating them.

September may prove to be physically taxing on both your emotions and your health. Don't take on more than your fair share of duties. Don't drudge or sacrifice yourself too much. Watch for drama and symptoms of the martyr complex. Be careful how you schedule yourself and keep your promises. Try to resist becoming involved in family arguments. Your family and friends will demand a great deal of attention, and you could become stubborn trying to maintain your position. If tensions have not been discussed or resolved, a troubled relationship may flounder between September and the end of the year. Solid relationships should strengthen and lovingly mature.

By October or November you should begin to realize you have worked things out to a more positive conclusion; pointing towards more time to yourself next year. When necessary, take care of home and family matters, but explain to your family that you need some time to yourself. Take time to carefully finish projects that are important to you.

In November, you may have to make a major decision about domestic or family issues. Start a disciplined health regimen and stick to it. This is not a time for vacations or undisciplined behavior. You may have to serve on a jury. This is a year when progress is calculated by emotional generosity, and by the end of the year, expect bread cast upon the waters to return. Money that has been coming for some time finally arrives. Buy something that will last.

As the year closes it brings a time of great accomplishment and satisfaction. Rewards come through financial gain or through love and admiration of the opposite sex.

## January Vibrations (6 PY)

This month gives you an opportunity to spend time alone, to analyze and clarify your goals, to learn from the past, and to plan for the future. You may enlist the aid of professionals (lawyers, therapists, doctors, counselors) or look into religious or metaphysical studies. You'll seem to be drawn to the unusual and you may learn something of significance for the future.

Instead of taking action this month, wait and analyze current legal dealings, questionable relationships, and future plans or goals. Family matters will come to the forefront and changes you hadn't anticipated may come into effect. You should have a broad-minded, analytical, and critical point of view. But watch that you don't become too intellectual, thinking only from your mind, remember to use your heart, too. Financial matters may have you stressed and you'll have to spend time trying to gain a better understanding of your domestic affairs.

This isn't the month to be aggressive, sociable, or to pursue commercial ambitions. Think before speaking and examine the opinions of others carefully. Don't take what others say as gospel unless you are sure. Be a little secretive and don't reveal your thoughts.

Take time to be alone, read, study, research, write, teach, or enjoy philosophical conversations. Wait for the telephone to ring instead of being the one to call. This month you must be patient, tolerant, and willing to spend time alone. Spend some time in the country or change your diet and exercise. Go for long walks and hikes in nature.

Take care of your health. If possible make time to get a physical or dental checkup if something doesn't feel right. You may have to count on family members to assist you if you're not feeling up to par.

## February Vibrations (6 PY)

Although this month provides an opportunity for you to take control of business and financial matters, domestic and family obligations will begin to come to the forefront. You must rely on yourself, be forceful, self-confident, and act decisively.

Try to approach matters in a businesslike manner, dress with dignity, and express yourself with authority. You will have more ability to make things happen with regard to business or financial matters than in any other month. Family members may be called upon to assist you with a new opportunity that comes your way.

Family matters may conflict with your business ventures and forcing you to take time away from business to attend to domestic obligations. Keep your emotions in tact and do what is needed to move forward. You'll have to make a major decision involving money. It will be important for you not to procrastinate. You may have to approach family members for financial assistance. Opportunities for advancement, recognition, financial improvement, and business expansion are there, but only happen if you are organized, tactful, and persuasive. Associate with high-powered and enterprising people to help you take advantage of the opportunities.

If you advertise and promote the projects you started eight or nine months ago, exceptional results will be achieved. Adjustments with regard to business and domestic matters will have to be considered. Hard work and long hours may strain personal relationships. This isn't the time for vacations or undisciplined behavior. However, it will be important for you to take some breaks during this stressful time period to relieve the tension and pressure you feel.

## March Vibrations (6 PY)

This month gives you an opportunity to complete projects, be charitable, tolerant, and compassionate. Use this time to help others, to be generous, kind, and inspire or counsel those who are in need of your support. Try to give of yourself with little thought of reward. At times, situations will arise requiring you to have an unselfish, broad-minded attitude. Give blood, visit the elderly, needy, or sick and take a book, a treat, or a listening ear.

The projects, activities, or relationships that began eight or nine months ago are either completed or abandoned, causing you to readjust to different circumstances. This isn't the time to begin anything new or to force your will on others. Business affairs that come to an end will leave you with an unexpected sense of relief.

On the other hand, if a personal relationship is ending, strong emotions are likely. The ending will likely be connected to much drama. Try to be understanding and compassionate regardless of the situation. Remain sensitive and keep your feelings under control. Difficult as that may be, keeping feelings balanced will help to avoid misunderstandings and needless quarrels. Discuss problems with loved ones to clarify feelings and motivations. Listen and make sure you understand what the other person is saying to you. Examine your domestic situation thoroughly and initiate some changes you feel are necessary.

Take a long-distance trip if it's within your budget. This month can be used to meet with notable or helpful people who have the contacts or abilities to help further your ambitions. Your reputation may be enhanced by group interactions, auditions, and public appearances. Express yourself artistically, using your imagination, intuition, and inspiration for artistic creation. Write, paint, play a musical instrument, sing, or learn a new recipe.

### April Vibrations (6 PY)

This is the month to initiate changes or additions with regard to family or domestic matters. You've spent time contemplating, this is the time to put those thoughts into action. This will be an active month, full of new people, situations, and ideas. This is definitely the time to start a new activity, friendship, or vocation. You may meet someone with whom you'll have an important relationship, adding a positive note to your domestic life.

Carefully breaking down old conditions could cause a significant change to come into effect, bringing new solutions to some old problems. Be sensitive and caring when dealing with others, taking into consideration their needs and feelings. Quite possibly the changes taking place in your life will eventually draw you closer to loved ones, including siblings and parents. You may see yourself differently. Take the initiative to move yourself forward because now you're in the driver's seat and it's up to you to act.

This month things get accomplished that were on the brink of completion three months ago but didn't materialize. Be aggressive and make changes, although you will have to keep in mind that family obligations must be attended to in order for everything to run smoothly. Take the necessary steps to strengthen weak areas. Base your decisions on independent and intellectual evaluations because you probably won't get any help or encouragement from others. Take a chance if the odds are in your favor. Use originality and creativity, but don't go overboard and irritate or alienate others. If the time is right, investigate the possibility of buying or selling property, remodeling or redecorating your home. Be yourself and emphasize your abilities.

# 6 PERSONAL YEAR VIBRATION

## May Vibrations (6 PY)

This month offers an opportunity for you to interact with friends and lovers and to make others happy. Although you feel the urge to act, this isn't the time to be ambitious or to make any material changes. Instead, this is a time for you to work quietly, to take care of the details that may slow you down later. There may be some unexpected diversions that require patience on your part. Wait for developments, even though it may seem as though nothing is happening.

Rest and allow friends, lovers, and business associates time to think and adjust to things that may differ from their personal desires. Love, affection, and romance are likely to be offered by someone you hold dear. If someone needs a shoulder to cry on, offer yours. Be sensitive and willing to help those you love and care about. You may have to compromise and do the little things that you overlooked last month. Use this month to cooperate with friends and relatives while working on your projects. A friend or family member may need assistance with regard to financial or legal matters.

At times, situations arise that require you to be diplomatic, considerate, and tactful. Don't force issues. Be open-minded as you listen to others' sly remarks or constructive criticisms that may prove to be helpful. You may be overly sensitive and self-conscious, taking what others say the "wrong way" and end up with hurt feelings. Don't be that way. Try to be adaptable, understanding, and courteous while you wait for developments.

## June Vibrations (6 PY)

This month you will have an opportunity to feel happy, cheerful, playful, and self-expressive. The delays you experienced last month are taken care of and things seem to be moving along nicely. Use this month to enjoy friends, to entertain and be entertained. You'll have an active social life and you'll be invited to attend parties or social functions with old and new friends. Situations will arise requiring you to have an attractive appearance and to put on a happy face. This is a good month to take a short vacation or to travel to an out-of-the-way place for adventure and fun. Take the kids along if it's appropriate.

Call friends you haven't talked to in awhile; take a phone number at a party and make a new contact. The friends you meet may open doors to new opportunities. Shop for new clothes or decorate your home, but expect to lose money through frivolousness and extravagance. It's best to leave your credit card behind.

The projects you began four months ago will start to bloom. Use this month to talk about your ideas, show off your talents, and have fun with friends, lovers, and coworkers. All forms of communication will be important. Express yourself, use imagination, intuition, and inspiration in creative activities. Don't fall prey to negative thoughts or worry. This is a month to do something creative, so write, dance, sing, paint, cook, or play a musical instrument. Take time to have some fun!

### July Vibrations (6 PY)

This month, through hard work, you'll have an opportunity to produce substantial results and build for the future. You must seriously apply yourself with regard to money, routines, and physical fitness. This month isn't the time to be lazy, disorganized, or impractical. Instead, you must use this month to reconstruct plans or projects and take care of any mistakes in finance or judgment. Put everything in order to get ventures under way. Situations will arise that demand a straightforward approach. Research your ideas and don't gamble on the unknown.

At times, you'll probably feel limited or restricted. It's important that you take time to analyze the limitations or restrictions and see whether they are of your own making. If so, plan to eliminate them. You might have to change your point of view. An "attitude adjustment" could be in store. Some limitations are unchangeable and you'll have to learn how to deal with them in a more satisfactory manner.

Domestic responsibility is ever present this year, and this month you might have to take on additional work around the house. Repairs, rebuilding or remodeling will need to be attended to. Work instead of talking about what needs to be done. Be efficient and stabilize your finances. There may be legal matters for you to take care of. Offer to lend a hand to family members or close relatives if they need help with their chores. Sometimes all someone needs is a person to talk to for comfort and guidance. Follow through on commitments, organize time, and above all don't waste your energy. This is a time to throw silly notions out the window and be practical.

You may feel a bit stressed, so remember to take care of your health. If any health matters are affecting you, make time to see a doctor.

### August Vibrations (6 PY)

This month offers surprises and unexpected activities. You'll have an opportunity to expand your horizons, to progress, and make changes. You should get out and meet new people, see new places, experience new activities, and have unusual opportunities. Whimsical ideas, travel, and a drive toward less responsibility are in the air. In fact, if you travel, you may find strange or unexpected possibilities.

Some of the domestic changes you initiated earlier in the year are starting to take hold. The changes bring with them a sense of freedom allowing you to do the things you want to do regarding your home life. Although you're trying to minimize responsibilities, don't ignore your domestic obligations. Watch legal commitments and expect conflicts and outbursts.

Take a chance on luck and love, although love affairs may not last. Situations will arise requiring you to follow a hunch. If the odds are in your favor, take a chance. Be venturesome and don't be afraid of the future. Try something different, spontaneous, and dress to attract attention. Begin an exercise regimen. You'll feel restless. Try to channel your energy in a positive direction and be careful not to run yourself ragged. If you lack focus, you'll become unreliable, temperamental, and frustrated. Unexpected possibilities are around every corner, so be flexible, broad-minded, and full of energy.

## September Vibrations (6 PY)

This month gives you an opportunity to pay attention to loved ones and domestic duties and responsibilities. You'll have a chance to enjoy the deep pleasures of love and romance. Be sure to maintain peaceful relationships, make domestic improvements, and be emotionally responsive. You can enjoy sharing chores and good times with close family members, relatives or friends. Take time to enjoy children and to actively participate in children's activities.

Express your feelings openly and honestly. Communicating your intentions clearly to those you love will bring pleasurable rewards. The time is right to settle down, deepen love, and create harmony. This is a very good time to enjoy the pleasures of romance, love, and marriage.

If married, this could be a time to deepen your love and affection by renewing your wedding vows. Keep your emotions in balance and show a great deal of affection. In fact, the more love you give, the more you will receive. Take time to spend romantic and intimate moments with the one you love to help strengthen your bond.

On the other hand, if your marriage or personal relationship is not the way you want it to be, things could become tense. Problems will surface and issues will have to be dealt with. This is the month to resolve differences in your marriage, and decide whether you want to continue or end the relationship. Make an extra effort to talk over and resolve underlying issues and problems so that they won't get in the way of the relationship at a later date. Find a comfortable way to deal with limitations or restrictive feelings you may have toward each other.

If you're contemplating marriage, discuss all the intricacies of the marital bond you want to form, weighing all aspects as they relate to your relationship. Now is the time to be honest and up-front when discussing your future together. Don't be stubborn, intolerant, or worrying. Let your feelings be known; discuss what you expect or want from a marriage or serious commitment. Be mature, devoted, and trustworthy when dealing with emotions.

At times, situations will arise that require you to sacrifice some of your personal desires. Use this month to be of service and assistance to those who need you. Give of yourself without the martyr syndrome coming into play. Take time to teach, pacify, and indicate approval. Through serving others, including children, you may find doors opening to new opportunities. Be willing to help those who need it in order to gain a sense of satisfaction. Harboring ill will or resentment will only cause problems. Others can sense if you don't really want to help them, or feel they are imposing on your good nature. Forget the drama and help someone out of the goodness of your heart.

This month, amid the hurly-burly of domestic activities and obligations, try to find time to use your imagination and express yourself creatively. Write, paint, cook, or play a musical instrument. The focus on this month is to provide a peaceful, happy, and beautiful environment in your home. This is your domestic month, don't travel unless you're going to visit family. If you do decide to take a vacation, the obligations you left behind will be there with a vengeance when you get back.

## October Vibrations (6 PY)

This month gives you an opportunity to spend time alone and analyze the changes you've been involved in this year. It's a time to review your accomplishments and to clarify your goals. Learn from the past and make some plans for the future. Are there still some domestic obligations or problems that you need to pay closer attention to? You may enlist the aid of professionals (lawyers, therapists, counselors) or look into religious or metaphysical studies. Figure out what it is you want to do when next year arrives. What would you like to accomplish? Think about taking a college class next year or some course of study you're interested in. You'll seem to be drawn to the unusual and you may learn something of significance for the future.

Instead of taking action this month, wait and analyze current legal dealings, questionable relationships, and future plans or goals. You should have a broad-minded, analytical, and critical point of view. Watch that you don't become too intellectual, thinking only from your mind. When deciding what to do, remember to use your heart, too.

This isn't the month to be aggressive, sociable, or to pursue commercial ambitions. Think before speaking and examine the opinions of others carefully. Don't take what others say as gospel unless you are sure. Be a little secretive; don't reveal your thoughts. However, it may be necessary to discuss your need to spend time alone with family members or those close to you so that they don't end up feeling left out or neglected. Let them know it isn't them, it's you who needs to take some time to be alone.

Take time to be alone, read, study, research, write, teach, or enjoy philosophical conversations. Wait for the telephone to ring instead of being the one to call. This month you must be patient, tolerant, and willing to spend time alone. If possible, spend some time in the country or change your diet and exercise. Go for long walks. Take care of your health and, if possible, schedule a checkup.

## November Vibrations (6 PY)

This month, business ventures and family obligations will need to be taken care of. Contracts, negotiations, and agreements related to your home will come to the forefront. You should rely on yourself, be forceful, and self-confident. You will progress if you act decisively, approach matters in a businesslike manner, dress with dignity, and express yourself with authority. You have an opportunity to take control and make things happen with regard to business or financial matters. This isn't the time for vacations or undisciplined behavior.

You'll have to make a major decision involving money. Tax or insurance affairs will need to be dealt with. It will be important for you not to procrastinate. A close friend or relative may have private legal or financial difficulties and you will be urgently called upon for assistance. Your own business ventures may require an extra effort on your part, either with your time or money. Conflicts arise during this busy month and it will be up to you to clarify which responsibilities are yours, which ones you can comfortably carry, and which ones you can't help with. Be realistic when appraising the situations placed before you and discuss the options with those who are directly involved. Staying calm during this unsettled time will be difficult, but keep strong feelings under control. Misunderstandings can result when feelings are not clearly discussed.

Opportunities for advancement, recognition, financial improvement, and business expansion are there, but only happen if you are organized, tactful, and persuasive. Associate with high-powered and enterprising people to help you take advantage of the opportunities.

If you advertise and promote the projects you started eight or nine months ago, exceptional results will be achieved. Hard work and long hours may strain personal relationships.

## December Vibrations (6 PY)

As the year draws to a close, this month gives you an opportunity to complete projects, be charitable, tolerant, and compassionate. Use the holiday season to help others, to be generous, kind, and inspire or counsel those who are in need of your support. Be a Santa Claus. Try to give of yourself with little thought of reward. At times, situations will arise requiring you to have an unselfish, broad-minded attitude. Give blood, visit the elderly, needy, or sick and take a book, a treat, or a listening ear.

Some of the projects, activities, or relationships that began earlier during the year are either completed or abandoned, causing you to readjust to different circumstances. Although the endings will likely be connected to much drama and strong emotions, you may be surprised to feel a sense of freedom and relief. Try to be understanding and compassionate regardless of the situation. Clear up misunderstandings and approach all matters with sensitivity. This isn't the time to begin anything new or to force your will on others. Try to keep in mind that endings allow for new beginnings and make it easier for you to move into new directions, relationships, and experiences next year.

Take a long-distance trip if it's within your budget. This month can be used to meet with notable or helpful people who have the contacts or abilities to help further your ambitions. Enjoy holiday festivities with close friends, relatives, and other special people in your social circle. Show appreciation to all those who have helped you during the year. Create a feeling of well-being. Your reputation may be enhanced by group interactions, auditions, and public appearances. Express yourself artistically, using your imagination, intuition, and inspiration for artistic creation. Write, paint, sing, play a musical instrument, learn to cook a new dish.

# 7 PERSONAL YEAR VIBRATION

For most people, this will be a slow year, filled with communication delays, unexpected feelings of loneliness, and legal questions. For others, the year focuses on some specialized course of study you decided upon last October. You'll find yourself researching, studying, and analyzing either alone or as a member of a group. These studies can lead to business improvement or perhaps a new career.

There will be money to be made, and recognition will be yours; however, you won't receive the return or financial reward you feel you deserve. Watch that you are not drawn into illegal or dishonest affairs, as these are likely to surface two years from now, causing you much grief, embarrassment, and loss.

As you search for self-discovery you may be led into deep religious studies, psychology, metaphysical investigation, or scientific research. You'll have heightened sensitivity and an ability to think clearly and deeply. Basically, it's time for self-examination, meditation, introspection, and getting yourself together. You'll likely have a desire to know more and to specialize your knowledge and talents.

This will be an introspective year. You'll feel the need to look over the past and plan for the future. The past five or six years have been full of activity and turmoil, and now is the time for personal peace as you seek access to life's great mysteries.

You may have a desire to spend more time alone, to get away from the hustle and bustle of daily living. If you are able to do this, it will be to your advantage to rest, improve your mind and health. This year gives you the opportunity to discover what you enjoy doing the most. Pay attention to your thoughts and follow your inner urges. If there's a course of study you wanted to pursue in the past but couldn't, this could be the time for you to go for it. This year, what you think will be very important.

Instead of fighting for your rights, arguing, or attempting to explain, you'll be better off if you remain quiet or say very little. This will be a very important year for you and so much depends on a right state of mind. You'll have a strong tendency to spend a lot of time brooding, searching for happiness. Don't brood over the past, just look it over and be done with it. Try to direct your energies and abilities outward, to a more positive direction. It will be important for you to curb impulsiveness, particularly in emotional matters.

Since you'll be involved in a good deal of ongoing work you may experience feelings of limitation. Let everything pertaining to business stay where it is. This isn't the year for business expansion or for starting new ventures. Use this time for reflection and perfection, and for putting the finishing touches on things you began earlier. As long as you don't rush out after money, this may be a good financial year. Wait for developments, even though it seems as if nothing is happening.

During the year you'll approach a time of shifting values. Take time to pause, look back, and analyze what you have been working on for the past six years. Observe what no longer works in your life. Who and what have you outgrown? It seems as though you're searching for new friends and contacts with others with similar intellectual needs. You may have to let go of something of value; have faith that it will return to you in its own time.

The year will be filled with many interesting and unusual experiences as you will be drawn to interests and activities you never thought of before. You may be drawn into research to develop ideas, formulas, or theories for books, presentations, or teachings. Even though you feel isolated and without control, try to remember you're laying a foundation for inner peace and strength which will make big changes in your life later. Do your best to avoid periods of prolonged withdrawal and depression. Use positive thinking to chase away the blues. Whatever happens will be for the best. Learn the meaning of faith

The year will be lonely in many respects and you may have to learn to be comfortable with yourself. During times when you experience bouts of loneliness or feeling all alone, try to relate more to others, to feel that others care. You may be feel bored with crowds and social activities, preferring to be by yourself so you can study and read. Don't let feelings get out of hand. For some people, this will be difficult.

You'll appear to be on a different wavelength, and your withdrawn manner may make it difficult for friends, family, and associates to approach you. Your desire to understand yourself, an argumentative attitude, or self-centeredness may be misunderstood by others who may criticize or condemn you because you seem so determined to think for yourself, or make better use of your mind. Although it will be difficult for you to clearly explain yourself (you probably won't understand yourself or why you're acting this way either), you must consider others, for if you are not careful, you may alienate the people you really care about.

On the other hand, associates, friends, and family may be hard to understand and you may experience unreasonableness in others. Take a moment to look at yourself and make sure you're not unreasonable yourself. If you root things out logically, with fairness and understanding, you will find unexpected rewards. Allow others to work things out for themselves too.

In a 7 year, many marriages can either flounder or prosper by reaching higher plateaus of understanding and love. If there is a conflict of goals, marriage will not be easy. Talk about misunderstandings and rework agreements rather than give in to fiery outbursts. If you are tempted to have an affair, be aware that the affair will come to light two years from now.

This is not the ideal year to marry, divorce, or make major purchases. Try not to draw conclusions or take action; keep spiritual and intellectual values in mind. If you can, use discretion and wait until this year ends to make major decisions. Take a good look at realistically perfecting your desires. What is it you really want out of life? Try to avoid any feelings of confusion, repression, or humiliation. There really are no limitations or restrictions which can't be overcome through faith and peace. Just don't try too hard or force issues.

If you use the right methods, this year can bring you recognition and financial rewards in spite of all the problems. Too many changes and restlessness can cause delays and you might miss an important opportunity. It will be very important for you to remember that the grass isn't always greener on the other side. The most promising plans will work out whether or not you take control. In fact, if aggressive actions are taken, incoming financial and material activities will be delayed. The Universe knows best. Wait until the time is right. Whether or not you understand how things will happen for the best isn't important right now; expect the best, have faith, and take a break from outside responsibilities and ambitions. You may end up growing more spiritually than materially this year.

This year presents a time for you to develop new interests and deeper understandings. Intuition will play an important part in your life, and if you listen to your thoughts for guidance, you should be able to understand yourself and others better. The direction you take may have to be taken on instinct. Go with your gut reaction. You may feel a lot of confusion, negativity, and frustration. If you reason things out, gain understanding, and deal fairly with others, your intuition could even bring you recognition.

Remember to take care of your health, too. Next year will be a time for you to actively pursue commercial or material ambitions, so take care of yourself now. If possible, plan medical and dental checkups during the early part of the year. Use this year wisely and don't ignore any physical discomforts; discuss any and all problems with your doctor or dentist. Watch what you eat and be cautious toward stimulants and spicy foods.

### Personal Month Vibrations in a 7 Personal Year

The following is a brief outline of the vibrations you can expect during the 7 Personal Year (for a more detailed description of what a specific month has in store for you, read the information found under the month heading, at the end of this section).

Use January and February to completely release the emotional residue of last year. Expenses will be high and you may experience disappointments involving large sums of money. February could be a very trying and emotional month. There may be unexpected rewards or disappointments. Reflect on your life and reevaluate your plans and goals.

March brings a time for personal values, noncommercial focuses, and self-analysis. Success revolves around your special talent or skill. Take time to learn something new about something old. After all, you don't know it all. You need solitude, understanding, and wisdom in order to mature.

In April, use your intuition as it may unconsciously lead you to the right place. Be a perfectionist. Money could be a problem, and it seems you have to wait for everything. You may be asked to give up something.

Money issues become less pressing during May. Shop for new clothes and decorate your home, but watch that you don't overspend. Commercial ambitions or physical strains are not favored during the spring and summer months.

Schedule medical and dental checkups in June. Reconstruct plans or projects and take care of any mistakes in finance or judgment. Don't let feelings of frustration, limitation or restriction get the best of you.

During July you'll experience a great deal of inner growth. Before you start to argue, examine your motives and be sure you are communicating your intentions clearly. Restlessness, or a need for stimulation from others could interfere with your introspective goals. Spend the remainder of the year becoming attuned to your inner self and environment.

August gives you an opportunity to pay attention to loved ones. Maintain peaceful relationships, make domestic improvements, and be emotionally responsive.

During September, you will probably question your goals and life-style very seriously. Use your intuition and get in touch with your higher self. Try not to be inflexible, shy, or retiring. Family and friends may be confused or alienated because you seem to be on a "different" wavelength. Be careful about over-stimulation and fatigue. Instead of taking action, wait and analyze current legal dealings, questionable relationships, and future plans or goals. Think before speaking and you should be a little secretive. Don't reveal your thoughts. Spend time in the country if you can and be patient with money.

October brings some activity related to business affairs. Put some of the year's awareness into practice by using a practical and realistic approach.

During November a personal or business relationship may flounder or come to an end. Try to stay calm.

The holiday season brings new opportunities. At times you may feel lonely or isolated and will need lots of support and encouragement from others. Do things as well as possible and take care of all the details. You may have to give up something of value. This could be a trying time in terms of money, so watch your spending. Get a new hairstyle, visit a new place, join a church, or meet a new friend who shares a special interest of yours. Try to keep a smile on your face and be patient. Take some time to enjoy family and friends.

## January Vibrations (7 PY)

This month gives you an opportunity to take care of any loose ends in business and financial matters. Make the effort to clean up ventures now so that they won't come back to haunt you at a later date. You may want to pass some of your domestic duties on to other family members. This year you'd rather spend time investigating interesting subjects than taking on more business or domestic responsibilities. You will probably feel like phasing out some of your projects, especially the ones that don't seem like they're going anywhere.

You'll have to make a major decision involving money. It will be important for you not to procrastinate. Try to structure and stabilize your finances so that you'll be able to manage your affairs this year without putting too much emphasis on money matters.

Opportunities for recognition and financial improvement are there, but only happen if you are organized, tactful, and persuasive. Although new opportunities may present themselves, keep in mind that they'll probably hold little possibility for you this year. If you advertise and promote the projects you started eight or nine months ago, you may achieve some beneficial results. Hard work and long hours may strain personal relationships. Tell those close to you how you feel and let them in on some of your introspective plans for the year.

## February Vibrations (7 PY)

This month gives you an opportunity to complete the projects or relationships that weren't getting you anywhere. Be charitable, tolerant, and compassionate, using this time to help others. Be generous, kind, and inspire or counsel those who are in need of your support. Try to give of yourself with little thought of reward. At times, situations will arise requiring you to have an unselfish and broad-minded attitude.

The projects, activities, or relationships that began eight or nine months ago are either completed or abandoned, causing you to readjust to different circumstances. Close relationships or long-time friendships (either business or personal) may leave you now, but you'll probably feel comfortable with the separations. More than likely some of these people will return to your life later. The separations and endings will likely be connected to much drama and strong emotions. Try to be understanding and compassionate regardless of the situation. This isn't the time to begin anything new or to force your will on others. Instead, be sensitive to the needs and feelings of others, as well as to your own. As the month draws to a close you start to feel the need to spend more time in solitude.

It might be a good idea to clarify your own feelings, although you might not know exactly where you're headed this year. Talk with others and discuss your feelings so they have some understanding of what's on your mind and what you're going through.

Take a long-distance trip if it's within your budget. This month can be used to meet with notable or helpful people who have the contacts or abilities to help further your ambitions. Your reputation may be enhanced by group interactions, auditions, and public appearances. Express yourself artistically, using your imagination, intuition, and inspiration for artistic creation. Write, paint, sing, play a musical instrument, or learn to cook a new dish.

## March Vibrations (7 PY)

This month will be active, full of new people, situations, and ideas. A change may come into effect, bringing new solutions to some old problems. Take the initiative to spend quiet time by yourself and move forward on some of the ideas for study or research you thought about at the beginning of the year. You'll be put in the driver's seat. It's up to you to act on your wants, needs, and desires.

Now is the time to learn about the things you've wanted to know about but hadn't had the opportunity to do so yet.

This month things get accomplished that were on the brink of completion three months ago but didn't materialize. Break up old conditions you don't like and strengthen weak areas. Base your decisions on independent and intellectual evaluations because you probably won't get any help or encouragement from others. Contemplate or meditate on the things you feel are worth your time and effort. You may see yourself differently.

Take a chance if the odds are in your favor. Be yourself and emphasize your abilities. Use originality and creativity, but don't go overboard and irritate or alienate others. You might not get as much alone time as you'd like, but you'll feel satisfied that you're headed in the right direction.

### April Vibrations (7 PY)

This month offers a chance for you to interact with people who are interesting, intriguing, and who have unusual occupations. It's an excellent time for religious or metaphysical study or research. Investigate intellectual matters that stir your curiosity. You'll have an opportunity to expand and develop your psychic powers. If you take time to meditate or pray, you may be given some special high-level awareness. Tune into yourself, listen to your thoughts, and be open to receive. If you feel comfortable discussing these types of things with your close friends and family members, go ahead and share some of the important insights and understandings you get.

Although you feel the urge to act, this isn't the time to be ambitious or to make any material changes. Instead, this is a time for you to work quietly, to take care of the details that may slow you down later. Wait patiently for developments, even though it may seem as though nothing is happening.

Rest and allow friends, lovers, and business associates time to think and adjust to things that may differ from their personal desires. At times, situations arise that require you to be diplomatic, considerate, and tactful. Don't force issues. Instead, use patience and sensitivity when dealing with both old and new friends. You may have to compromise and do the little things that you overlooked last month. Use this month to cooperate with others while working on your projects, or help others with their ventures.

Be open-minded as you listen to others' sly remarks or constructive criticisms that may prove to be helpful. You may be overly sensitive and self-conscious, taking what others say the "wrong way" and end up with hurt feelings. Don't be that way. Try to be adaptable, understanding, and courteous. Remember you're working on a different wavelength this year and others probably don't understand what's going on with you.

## May Vibrations (7 PY)

Although this month offers you a chance to get out and party with your friends, you will probably feel more like spending time with smaller groups of people. In fact, you might find you'd rather spend quality time with a few, choice friends who are into investigating and learning about the same types of things that you're interested in.

May's vibrations give you an opportunity to feel happy, cheerful, playful, and self-expressive. Situations will arise requiring you to have an attractive appearance and to put on a happy face. If you have an opportunity to travel, take a short vacation if it fits in with your current study program. Taking a trip to an out of the way place may provide some specific insights in the areas of study you're currently involved with or interested in.

Call old friends you haven't talked to in awhile; take a phone number at a party and make a new contact. Spend happy times with the one you love or have a romantic interest in. New friends you meet may open doors to investigations and studies you haven't thought of or perhaps haven't even heard of before.

Shop for new clothes or decorate your home, but expect to lose money through frivolousness and extravagance. It's best to leave your credit card behind and buy only what you can afford.

The projects you began four months ago will start to bloom. Use this month to talk about your ideas, show off your talents, and have fun with friends, lovers, and coworkers. All forms of communication will be important. Take some time to express yourself, using your imagination, intuition, and inspiration in creative activities. Be creative, have fun and enjoy yourself!

## June Vibrations (7 PY)

This month, through hard work, you'll have an opportunity to produce substantial results and build for the future. You must seriously apply yourself with regard to money, routines, and physical fitness. This month isn't the time to be lazy, disorganized, or impractical. Instead, you must use this month to reconstruct plans or projects and take care of any mistakes in finance or judgment. Put everything in order to get studies or research projects under way. Situations will arise that demand a straightforward approach. Research your ideas and don't gamble on the unknown.

At times, you'll probably feel limited or restricted. When you feel overly burdened, it's time to take a break. Take time to analyze the limitations or restrictions and see whether they are of your own making. If so, plan to eliminate them. You might have to change your point of view or a fixed attitude that just isn't getting you anywhere. Some limitations are unchangeable and you'll have to learn how to deal with them in a more satisfactory manner.

Although it may not appeal to you, you might be asked to take on more domestic responsibility. Take care of your duties, work instead of talking about what needs to be done. Be efficient and stabilize your finances. Follow through on commitments, organize time, and above all don't waste your energy. New ventures may not have potential for you, so don't waste time and effort pursuing things that don't fit in with what's going on in your life now.

Legal matters, contracts, or agreements may have you feeling a bit stressed. Make a commitment to yourself to spend some time meditating and getting your body in shape. Regular physical exercise will prove to be beneficial and a step in the right direction with regard to taking care of your health. This is a time to throw silly notions out the window and be practical.

### July Vibrations (7 PY)

This month offers you an opportunity to expand your horizons, to progress, and make changes. You should get out and meet new people, see new places, experience new activities, and have unusual opportunities. Explore new directions that interest you and pique your curiosity. Plan to work on your talents and abilities that you've ignored in the past.

Whimsical ideas, travel, and a drive toward less responsibility are in the air. In fact, if you travel, you may find unusual or unexpected possibilities. You want and need more freedom and stimulation. Getting away from the humdrum of your current existence and out into the world will give you a chance to relax and expand your horizons.

Try to minimize responsibilities if you can, but don't ignore them. Watch legal commitments and expect conflicts and outbursts. Take a chance on luck and love. You could meet someone special. Be careful with your feelings as love affairs may not last.

At times, situations will arise requiring you to follow a hunch. If the odds are in your favor, take a chance. Be venturesome and try something different or spontaneous. Pay attention to how you look, dress to attract attention, and get some exercise. Search out experiences that can stretch your mind. Be careful to limit your experiences, choosing only those you are really interested in investigating so that you don't run yourself ragged. If you lack focus, you'll become unreliable, temperamental, and frustrated. Stimulating possibilities are around every corner, so be flexible, broad-minded, and full of energy.

## August Vibrations (7 PY)

This month gives you an opportunity to pay attention to loved ones and home or community duties and responsibilities. This is your domestic month and the duties you'll have to take care of will likely interfere with your other activities. Be sure to maintain peaceful relationships, make domestic improvements, and be emotionally responsive. Most likely there will be some unexpected legal, financial, or family matters that you'll have to deal with. Close relatives could come to you with their problems, asking for your assistance. Don't travel unless you're going to visit family.

The focus on this month is to provide a peaceful, happy, and beautiful environment in your home. The time is right to settle down, deepen love, and create harmony. You can enjoy sharing chores and good times with family or close friends. Make time to enjoy children and to participate in children's activities.

This is a good month to enjoy the pleasures of romance, love, and marriage. Keep your emotions in balance and show a great deal of affection. In fact, the more love you give, the more you will receive. Be mature, devoted, and trustworthy when dealing with emotions. Don't be stubborn, intolerant, or worrying. All worry gets you is an ulcer.

At times, situations will arise that require you to sacrifice some of your personal desires. If asked to lend a hand, give of yourself without thought of reward. Through serving others you may find doors opening to new opportunities.

Make some time to use your imagination and express yourself artistically. Creative endeavors that you participate in (or make plans to do later) could lead to significant breakthroughs in your career. Write, paint, cook, sing, or play a musical instrument. Just do something to make use of your artistic talents and abilities.

## September Vibrations (7 PY)

This month, the full force of what this year has been about comes to center stage. You'll have a very strong need to spend this month alone, to analyze and clarify your goals. You'll think about the past and plan for the future. You may enlist the aid of professionals (lawyers, doctors, therapists, counselors). Look deeper into religious or metaphysical studies. For the better part of this year you've been drawn to the unusual. This month, through prayer and meditation, you could learn something of significance for the future. It's possible you'll receive a special spiritual illumination or understanding that will help to clarify your outlook.

Instead of taking action this month, wait and analyze current legal dealings, questionable relationships, and future plans or goals. Quite possibly one of the creative endeavors you took part in earlier this year will come to fruition, giving you much satisfaction. You should have a broad-minded, analytical, and critical point of view. But watch that you don't become too intellectual, thinking only from your mind, remember to use your heart, too. This is a time for inner growth and peace of mind.

This isn't the month to be aggressive, sociable, or to pursue commercial ambitions. Think before speaking and examine the opinions of others carefully. Don't take what others say as gospel unless you are sure. Be a little secretive; don't reveal your thoughts. Others may provoke you and start arguments or quarrels. Some of those you love and care about won't understand your private affairs and may have concerns about what you're doing. Try to be understanding and discuss problems or feelings of resentment with those close to you. Being sensitive to the feelings of others will help avoid misunderstandings.

Take time to be alone, read, study, research, write, teach, or enjoy philosophical conversations. Wait for the telephone to ring instead of being the one to call. This month you must be patient, tolerant, and willing to spend time alone. If possible, spend some time in the country or change your diet and exercise. Go for long walks. Take care of your health.

## October Vibrations (7 PY)

For the most part, this year has been relatively quiet as you've searched for answers. This month the pace changes considerably. Major business ventures probably won't get off the ground until next year; however, this month you'll have an opportunity to take control of some business and financial matters. In fact, this month you will have more ability to make things happen with regard to business or financial matters than you've had in any other month this year.

This is a time to rely on yourself, be forceful, self-confident, and act decisively. Approach all matters in a businesslike manner, dress with dignity, and express yourself with authority. You'll begin to feel the vibrations of the approaching 8 year. Be on the lookout for new business ventures or commercial activities that are compatible with your goals. Test new opportunities but don't invest too much of your time right now. It's better to adopt a wait and see attitude, at least until the potential has had more time to develop.

You'll have to make a major decision involving money. It will be important for you not to procrastinate. Opportunities for advancement, recognition, financial improvement, and business expansion are there, but only happen if you are organized, tactful, and persuasive. This isn't the time for vacations or undisciplined behavior. Use your time wisely and associate with high-powered and enterprising people to help you take advantage of the opportunities that come your way.

If you advertise and promote the projects you started eight or nine months ago, exceptional results will be achieved. Hard work and long hours may strain personal relationships.

## November Vibrations (7 PY)

This month gives you an opportunity to complete projects, be charitable, tolerant, and compassionate. Use this time to help others, to be generous, kind, and inspire or counsel those who are in need of your support. Try to give of yourself with little thought of reward. At times, situations will arise requiring you to have an unselfish, broad-minded attitude. Give blood, visit the elderly, needy, or sick and take a book, a treat, or a listening ear.

The projects, activities, or relationships that began eight or nine months ago are either completed or abandoned, causing you to readjust to different circumstances. Things seem to be coming together now. You'll begin to recognize the spiritual insights you've gained throughout the year and apply them to your ventures. You'll be amazed at your inner growth.

As projects or relationships begin to phase out, the endings will likely be connected to much drama and strong emotions. Keep your emotions in tact and under control. Try to be understanding and compassionate regardless of the situation. Even though you may not want things to end, especially if a romantic interest is terminating, realize that closure is a part of life and there is nothing you can do to change the inevitable. Endings happen, leaving you with more time and energy to pursue new ventures. This isn't the time to begin anything new or to force your will on others. Instead, help your friends or business associates deal with the closures in a calm manner.

Take a long-distance trip if it's within your budget. This month can be used to meet with notable or helpful people who have the contacts or abilities to help further your ambitions. Your reputation may be enhanced by group interactions, auditions, and public appearances. Express yourself artistically, using your imagination, intuition, and inspiration for artistic creation. Write, paint, play a musical instrument, learn to cook a new dish, or spend an afternoon singing.

## December Vibrations (7 PY)

The year has been slow and quiet, with your thoughts on contemplation and solitude. This month things will begin to change and you'll want to spend more time with friends and family. December will be active, full of new people, situations, and ideas.

This is definitely a time to start a new activity, friendship, or vocation. A change may come into effect, bringing new solutions to some old problems. Take the initiative to move yourself forward. You'll be put in the driver's seat. It's up to you to act and put some of your plans into action. Look into new business ventures that you feel are worth your time and energy. New opportunities could hold great potential for your personal gain, perhaps enhancing your reputation, status, and financial situation. Take a chance if the odds are in your favor. Be yourself and emphasize your talents and abilities.

This month things get accomplished that were on the brink of completion three months ago but didn't materialize. Don't be overly aggressive or try to force issues while you make changes. It's time to break up old conditions you don't like and strengthen weak areas. Base your decisions on independent and intellectual evaluations because you probably won't get any help or encouragement from others. Use originality and creativity, but don't go overboard and irritate or alienate others.

As the year draws to a close, you may see yourself differently. Rest and take a few moments to ponder the new insights and spiritual awareness you've gained and decide how you'll use them to benefit yourself and others in the following years.

# 8 PERSONAL YEAR VIBRATION

During the course of this year a major new opportunity will unfold, quite possibly you'll experience a significant change in your work environment. This is a year of action. Emphasis will be placed on travel, advancement, financial matters, social status, power, authority, business, and accomplishment. You'll have a chance to improve your professional standing, finances, and reputation, and will be recognized for your potential and skills. The year will bring promotions, advancement, and recognition for your contributions in the business world. You must act very businesslike, exercise good judgment, be practical and efficient throughout the year to reap the benefits.

Since your intuition and intelligence are greatly enhanced this year, you'll find yourself having many original ideas or inventions. You'll feel the need to start something new or to expand your present activities in a new and different way. Life will bring you in contact with people of importance. Carefully seek an outlet for your unique ideas, but don't be led into unprofitable associations through persuasive, eccentric, or unusual acquaintances. Wise judgment will bring you much in the way of wealth and prestige.

It will be very important for you to think of the future. Do not dwell on the past or mistakes. Plan a goal for yourself and go after it. The year calls for good judgment and a deeper understanding of human nature. Organization and reorganization will be required for success and advancement.

You will feel a great deal of mental strain in making ends meet and in accomplishing your goals. Quite possibly you'll be involved in two lines of work carried out at the same time. Don't become unstable or erratic. Feeling the need for recognition and power could cause you to fall prey to impulsive actions or "get-rich-quick" schemes. In order to succeed, you must earn your way honestly. By using your head wisely, combining reason and emotion to your plans or ideas, and turning the details over to others when necessary, you should see an improvement in status and finances by year's end.

For some, this year may bring feelings of inner hostility and resentment from simmering injured pride to the surface. You may feel you have deserved attention or recognition for some time and when the promotion finally comes, your pride and ego needs produce a vengeful, or reckless behavior. Avoid the evils of false pride. Instead, try to work out your internal conflicts and misunderstandings with others. It's time for you to find and establish your own identity, enhancing your natural abilities for inspiration and leadership.

This year can also bring frustration with authority. You'll find coworkers, friends, relatives, or lovers challenge your word on just about everything. It seems as though everyone is demanding something from you, either your time or your money. With so many problems it will be difficult for you to maintain and hold your position, adding to your physical and mental strain. Be careful of confrontations and watch your reactions. Don't attempt to win every argument, refuse to listen, nod politely in agreement, and then later criticize. If you become unconcerned with other's needs you may alienate associates and hurt your potential. The clue to growth this year is to be willing to learn from the people around you.

It will be important for you to balance power with compassion and consideration of others. You may become critical of those in charge and start to criticize supervisors or leaders in your business. Stop and look at yourself for a moment. You might realize that the misuse of power and authority you so readily see in others, and that troubles you so much, may also be in you. If you are helpful, rational, and cooperative with others, you'll find those in authority recognizing your abilities and opening doors. Handle any and all responsibilities with confidence and sensitivity.

Dealing with money will be particularly important this year. The amounts of money and power plays that come in or go out may be larger than what you have previously handled. During the year you'll find that income and expense are often equal. Old issues and debts from the past will begin to surface and you'll have to "pay the piper" before you can progress. It will be important for you not to strain after money. Instead, concentrate on your sense of dollar worth so you can increase your earnings and cash flow.

Maintain a healthy attitude toward money or you could end up losing it all, falling into bankruptcy. Try not to overestimate your ability or the value of whatever you are dealing with, especially investments, buying or selling real estate or property, and in making exchanges. Major money mistakes can be made if you're not careful; these mistakes can affect you for years to come.

This is a time to be businesslike, avoid sentiment and emotion. It's time for you to learn to control your spending. Helping your kids or close friends and relatives is one thing; enabling them by taking on their bills or giving an unsecured loan is another. Some children have a difficult time paying back their parents or relatives because, in the far recesses of their minds, they believe they deserve the help and are entitled to the money. If you make a loan to a family member, make sure the agreement and terms of repayment are fully understood by all involved.

Driving yourself too hard will upset your health. If you pursue money for power, greed, or love of riches it will slip through your fingers as quickly as it is earned. Money earned honestly and productively can grow, bringing greater dividends. This year the key words are balance and perspective. Know what your effort is worth.

If romance is your objective, healthy, wealthy and ambitious prospects will come into your life. Don't be too dominant and try to ignore trivial or petty problems. You'll find that having a businesslike attitude will prove to be helpful, both in personal relationships and business.

The year could bring a change of residence. Quite possibly you'll be involved in purchasing a home or property, or a new vehicle. Make sure you can afford what you buy. Think things through logically and don't overestimate your resources. Heed this warning or you could have financial difficulties later on down the road. Property matters will bring assets along with problems to be worked out.

This year, the laws of compensation require that you think of those less fortunate than you. If you have the opportunity, serve as a volunteer or actively participate in a worthwhile philanthropic organization. Your greatest reward may be in the satisfaction you receive by reaching out and helping others.

## Personal Month Vibrations in an 8 Personal Year

The following is a brief outline of the vibrations you can expect during the 8 Personal Year (for a more detailed description of what a specific month has in store for you, read the information found under the month heading, at the end of this section).

Finish projects before you start the year off, if anything is pending make every effort to complete it. Financial rewards may be surprising. At the beginning of the year, people will look to you for your authority and recognize your worth. Take the initiative and move full steam ahead. This year you can reap the rewards of what you started seven years ago. Be consistent. Don't be afraid of challenges and changes.

February brings a time for you to break up old conditions you don't like and strengthen any weak areas. Be yourself and emphasize your abilities. Rewards will be plentiful and you'll have more abundance than ever before in your life, but only if you work hard. You'll be working with institutions or groups, and with money. Ideas discussed and planned in February will see light in April.

March offers an opportunity for you to interact with friends and lovers and make others happy. Don't let nervous tension get in the way of progress. You'll find misguided emotions will put a strain on your health.

You may move or change your living conditions in the spring. Thinking about buying a new home or property in the country? Friends or associates open doors, presenting opportunities for advancement and recognition. You may be required to travel in order to bring in new business. A variety of options will start to materialize. Examine opportunities realistically, and put them to use. Work instead of talking about what needs to be done. Don't waste time or money on frivolous items; purchase something basic and watch your spending. Travel only on business and with a specific goal.

June sparks sensual activity. If the odds are in your favor, take a chance and invest in the unusual. Travel, stay at the best hotels, and dress to attract attention. This is a great time for business, advertise yourself and get out more. If possible, set up a meeting with a rich person and pick his or her brain. Watch yourself with regard to physical stimulation and don't go overboard on food, drink, drugs or sex.

July brings an adjustment between family members or business partnerships. This may be a time for you to make a major commitment. If marriage is the objective, it's time to get up the nerve and go after the one you want. Business affairs may take a back seat to domestic life for the time being. An inheritance or gift could bring in money. Work and responsibilities will keep you active during July, August, and September.

If you feel lonely, take time to rest, meditate, and watch your health. If you allow your business or career to dominate your life, you'll feel run down and disappointed. Study religion or metaphysics to find a new slant on some of your old beliefs. Take a break from the hustle and bustle of everyday living and do something nice for yourself.

During the first and last weeks of September there is an increase in activity, money and influential alliances. Finances should improve as new opportunities become available. Your authority will be tested and you will be asked to prove yourself. Reorganize your affairs. Exercise caution regarding financial matters or investments. You will have more ability to make things happen in regard to business or financial matters than in any other month. Associate with high-powered and enterprising people to help you take advantage of the opportunities.

October brings personal and financial conclusions. You will have an opportunity to complete projects, be charitable, compassionate, and prepare for additional endings in the coming year. Let go of a petty attitude that only hinders and blocks your energy. Repeated effort, good judgment, and efficient methods will bring rewards and the freedom you are looking for.

November brings new projects or expansion of business ventures. Excellent business opportunities will put you in the driver's seat. Now is the time to act on a major project. This month will be full of decisions, purchases, promotions, advances, new people, new situations and ideas. Quite possibly you'll be involved with heavy machinery, publications, or heroism. You will have incredible energy. Watch for a clash of wills and learn to discipline yourself.

The pace slows considerably in during the holiday season. You attract recognition. In December you may experience a let down feeling after a year of much accomplishment. The last two weeks of December may produce a strain as surprises, unconventional behavior, relationships and details bring frustrating restrictions. Now is the time for you to overcome limitations. A relationship will demand a great deal of attention. Work quietly and take care of details, although many details bring frustrating restrictions.

## January Vibrations (8 PY)

After the patient waiting and introspection of last year, you're ready for things to move a little faster. Even though you're ready to move full steam ahead, there are still some activities from last year that need closure.

This month gives you an opportunity to complete projects, be charitable, tolerant, and compassionate. Use this time to help others, to be generous, kind, and inspire or counsel those who are in need of your support. Try to give of yourself with little thought of reward. At times, situations will arise requiring you to have an unselfish, broad-minded attitude. Give blood, visit the elderly, needy, or sick and take a book, a treat, or a listening ear.

Some of the projects, activities, or relationships that began last year are either completed or abandoned, causing you to readjust to different circumstances. Endings are required so that you can move forward on new, progressive ventures, and to allow you more freedom in which to do so. The endings will likely be connected to much drama and strong emotions. Try to be understanding and compassionate regardless of the situation. This isn't the time to begin anything new or to force your will on others.

If your spouse needs some special attention, or your children want to spend time with you, it is important that you make, and take, time for them. This will be a busy year filled with business propositions and money matters. Don't add to the stress by creating problems in your home because you'd rather work on your projects than hang out with your family. You can avoid temporary breakups by keeping a level head and being there for the ones you love. You'll have plenty of time as the year progresses to concentrate on your business ventures. Use a portion of this month to be with loved ones.

Take a long-distance trip if it's within your budget. This month can be used to meet with notable or helpful people who have the contacts or abilities to help further your ambitions. Your reputation may be enhanced by group interactions, auditions, and public appearances. Express yourself artistically, using your imagination, intuition, and inspiration for artistic creation.

## February Vibrations (8 PY)

Now you're in the driver's seat. This month will be active, full of new people, situations, and ideas, definitely a time to start a new activity, friendship, or vocation. A change may come into effect, bringing new solutions to some old problems, take the initiative to move yourself forward. It's up to you to act.

This month things get accomplished that were on the brink of completion three months ago but didn't materialize. Your long-term projects are starting to come to life. Be aggressive and make changes necessary to move things forward. Break up old conditions you don't like and strengthen weak areas. Base your decisions on independent and intellectual evaluations because you probably won't get any help or encouragement from others. Organize your affairs and make sure to take care of things that could get in your way; reorganize if you have to.

Others may see you differently. There is the possibility of a raise in status or recognition for past efforts, bringing with it increased responsibility and financial rewards. Follow through on commitments and be sure to read all documents before you sign them. There may be some financial or legal matters regarding your home, property, or business that you'll have to deal with.

This month, take a chance if the odds are in your favor. Be yourself and emphasize your abilities. Use originality and creativity, but don't go overboard and irritate or alienate others.

If stress starts to get to you, take a break. Allow yourself some time to rest and relax in order to keep your mind sharp and focused.

## March Vibrations (8 PY)

This month offers an opportunity for you to interact with friends and lovers and to make others happy. Although you feel the urge to act, this isn't the time to be ambitious or to make any material changes. Instead, this is a time for you to work quietly, to take care of the details that may slow you down later. Wait patiently for developments, keeping your projects running smoothly. Things are moving along even though it may seem as though nothing is happening. Temporary delays and stoppages are necessary for growth.

Rest and allow friends, lovers, and business associates time to think and adjust to things that may differ from their personal desires. Be cooperative while working with coworkers or friends. At times, situations arise that require you to be diplomatic, considerate, and tactful. Don't force issues. Maintain a sensitive, peaceful and calm persona. Try to become aware of what others may be going through and do your best to understand them. You may have to compromise and do the little things that you overlooked last month.

Spend some time during the month socializing with friends. You may meet someone who will have a significant impact on your life. A new romantic interest could enter your social circle. This person might just be "the one." Take time to spend with children and enjoy playing with them.

Be open-minded as you listen to others' sly remarks or constructive criticisms that may prove to be helpful. You may be overly sensitive and self-conscious, taking what others say the "wrong way" and end up with hurt feelings. Don't be that way. Instead, try to ponder and focus on some of the important insights you gained last year. You might be able to use your special insights to help you through some of your troubles.

Learn the causes of your stress and anxiety and work to overcome your feelings so they don't hinder your progress. Use this month to cooperate with others while working on your projects, or help others with their ventures. Try to be adaptable, understanding, and courteous while you wait for developments.

## April Vibrations (8 PY)

This month you will have an opportunity to feel happy, cheerful, playful, and self-expressive. This is a month to enjoy friends, to entertain and be entertained.
You'll have an active social life. There will be many parties or social functions to attend, and energetic people to meet. Situations will arise requiring you to have an attractive appearance and to put on a happy face. If it's in your budget, this is a good

month to take a short vacation, travel, or throw a big party.

Call old friends you haven't talked to in awhile; take a phone number at a party and make a new contact. Romantic interludes add to your pleasure. The friends you meet may open doors to new opportunities or offer assistance with some of your ventures, which will benefit you financially and provide greater recognition in your field.

Keep an eye on your budget at all times during this month. Shop for new clothes or decorate your home, but expect to lose money through frivolousness and extravagance. It's best to leave your credit card behind. Think before writing the check or loaning large sums of money to relatives.

The projects you began four months ago will start to bloom. Find an imaginative or creative way to enhance your projects. Even a slight change can make a world of difference and improve things.

Use this month to talk about your ideas, show off your talents, and have fun with friends, lovers, and coworkers. All forms of communication will be important. Express yourself, use imagination, intuition, and inspiration in creative activities. Spend time with friends and make a date to check out cultural events, or get tickets to a concert or art festival. Write, dance, sing, paint or draw, cook, or play a musical instrument. Just be creative and have fun!

## May Vibrations (8 PY)

This month, through hard work, you'll have an opportunity to produce substantial results and build for the future. You must seriously apply yourself with regard to money, routines, and physical fitness. This month isn't the time to be lazy, disorganized, or impractical. Instead, you must use this month to reconstruct plans or reorganize projects and take care of any mistakes in finance or judgment. Put everything in order to get ventures under way so that you can realize your goals. Situations will arise that demand a straightforward approach. Research your ideas and don't gamble on the unknown.

Last month was fun, this month isn't. It seems that every time you turn around another detail crops up that you have to take care of. At times, you'll probably feel limited or restricted. It's important that you take time to analyze the limitations or restrictions and see whether they are of your own making. If so, plan to eliminate them. You might have to change your point of view. An "attitude adjustment" could be what you need. Some limitations are unchangeable and you'll have to learn how to deal with them in a more satisfactory manner.

Check on your budget and make sure of your financial situation. This month, along with the business matters that need adjustment, you might also have to take on more domestic responsibility. Work instead of talking about what needs to be done. If you start feeling discouraged, remember that you're laying a foundation for bigger and better things to come. Be efficient and stabilize your finances. Follow through on commitments, organize time, and above all don't waste your energy.

You may feel a bit stressed and under pressure, so remember to take care of your health. Realize that the heavy workload is temporary. Next month things will relax, so take care of details now that can slow you down later. This is a time to throw silly notions out the window and be practical.

### June Vibrations (8 PY)

This month offers you an opportunity to expand your horizons, to progress, and make changes. You should get out and meet new people, see new places, experience new activities, and have unusual opportunities. People you meet may help to further advance your business or career. If offered, utilize their special abilities or business acumen to help further one of your projects.

You'll feel freer that you did last month. Whimsical ideas, freedom, travel, and a drive toward less responsibility are in the air. In fact, if you travel, you may find unusual or unexpected possibilities. Take time off for a vacation if it's in your budget. Try something different, spontaneous, dress to attract attention, and get out and exercise. Drop the old and look for the new. Be careful not to run yourself ragged. Don't lack focus, becoming unreliable, temperamental, and frustrated.

Try to minimize responsibilities if you can, but don't ignore them. Watch legal commitments and expect conflicts and outbursts. Take a chance on luck and love, although love affairs may not last. If you're in a relationship, make time for a special romantic interlude.

Situations will arise requiring you to follow a hunch. If the odds are in your favor, take a chance and be venturesome. If a new business proposition comes your way, take time to check it out and, if you like what you see, begin to develop it. You should see many of your goals coming to fruition and you may be recognized for your accomplishments. It's time to be proud of yourself. Unexpected possibilities are around every corner, so be flexible, broad-minded, and full of energy.

### July Vibrations (8 PY)

This month gives you an opportunity to pay attention to loved ones and home or community duties and responsibilities. This is your domestic month and a time to sort out your priorities. Don't travel unless you're going to visit family. Be sure to maintain peaceful relationships, make domestic improvements, and be emotionally responsive. The time is right to settle down, deepen love, and create harmony.

Domestic duties may get in the way of your business ventures some time during the month. If so, ask for help from your family and see whether another family member can take over some of your chores so that you can devote your time to your business projects. Legal or insurance matters may have to be dealt with, especially if they pertain to your home and family.

This is a good month to enjoy the pleasures of romance, love, and marriage. Keep your emotions in balance and show a great deal of affection. In fact, the more love you give, the more you will receive.

At times, situations will arise that require you to sacrifice some of your personal desires. If someone close to you needs you for guidance or support, be there for them if at all possible. Make sure you spend enough time with your family and plan some fun activities for everyone. It is important that you make the time to be available to those you love and cherish.

Use this month to be of service. Give of yourself taking time to teach, pacify, and indicate approval. Through serving others you may find doors opening to new opportunities. Be mature, devoted, and trustworthy when dealing with emotions. Don't be stubborn, intolerant, or worrying.

This month also gives you a chance to use your imagination and express yourself artistically. Write, paint, cook, or play a musical instrument. The focus on this month is to provide a peaceful, happy, and beautiful environment in your home while continuing to work on your business ventures.

## August Vibrations (8 PY)

This month gives you an opportunity to spend time alone, to analyze and clarify your goals, to learn from the past, and to plan for the future. You may enlist the aid of professionals (lawyers, doctors, therapists, counselors) or look into religious or metaphysical studies. You'll be drawn to the unusual and through spiritual thought or insight, you may learn something of significance for the future.

Instead of taking action this month, wait and analyze current legal dealings, questionable relationships, and future plans or goals. You should have a broad-minded, analytical, and critical point of view. But watch that you don't become too intellectual, thinking only from your mind, remember to use your heart, too.

This isn't the month to be aggressive, sociable, or to pursue commercial ambitions. Instead, contemplate what's going on in your life. Are you heading in the right direction? Are your ventures progressing or reaching their potential? What things should you change or consider revamping? Think before speaking and examine the opinions of others carefully. Don't take what others say as gospel unless you are sure. Be a little secretive; don't reveal your thoughts.

Take time to be alone, read, study, research, write, teach, or enjoy philosophical conversations. If you take time away from your work, make sure colleagues know how to reach you so that your absence won't cause delays in business ventures.

Wait for the telephone to ring instead of being the one to call. This month you must be patient, tolerant, and willing to spend time alone. If possible, spend some time in the country or change your diet and exercise. Go for long walks. Take care of your health.

## September Vibrations (8 PY)

This month gives you an opportunity to dramatically move ahead. The time is right to take control of business and financial matters. You should rely on yourself, be forceful, self-confident, act decisively, approach matters in a businesslike manner, dress with dignity, and express yourself with authority. You will have more ability to make things happen with regard to business or financial matters than in any other month. This isn't the time for vacations or undisciplined behavior. Hard work and long hours may strain personal relationships.

You'll have to make a major decision involving money. It will be important for you not to procrastinate or vacillate. Think things through logically and make sure you can afford the payments of any loans or lines of credit offered to you. If you're the one offering the loan, make sure you can afford to lose the money if the loan is unsecured. Financial matters must be discussed and clearly understood by everyone involved. Make sure there are no misunderstandings with regard to repayment terms and conditions.

Opportunities for advancement, recognition, financial improvement, and business expansion are there, but only happen if you are organized, tactful, and persuasive. Associate with high-powered and enterprising people to help you take advantage of the opportunities.

If you advertise and promote the projects you started eight or nine months ago, exceptional results will be achieved. Perhaps a project you began years ago is finally paying off. Remember to thank and give credit to those individuals who helped you succeed.

### October Vibrations (8 PY)

This month offers another opportunity to complete projects, be charitable, tolerant, and compassionate. Use this time to help others, to be generous, kind, and inspire or counsel those who are in need of your support. Try to give of yourself with little thought of reward. At times, situations will arise requiring you to have an unselfish, broad-minded attitude. Give blood, visit the elderly, needy, or sick and take a book, a treat, or a listening ear.

The projects, activities, or relationships that began eight or nine months ago are either completed or abandoned, causing you to readjust to different circumstances. The transitions will likely be connected to much drama and strong emotions. Try to be understanding, sympathetic, and compassionate regardless of the situation. This isn't the time to begin anything new or to force your will on others. Try not to rock the boat and cause upsets between you and close friends or family members. This might not be the right time to part ways with a close friend. Cool off before you make a definite decision.

Take time to prepare yourself for major endings and changes that will come into effect next year. Contemplate which business ventures or personal relationships are beginning to show signs of terminating or changing in some way. Which projects, relationships, or activities do you want to begin to phase out of your life? Someone or something will be moving on and out of your life next year.

Take a long-distance trip if it's within your budget. It will probably do you good to get away from things for a few days. This month can be used to meet with notable or helpful people who have the contacts or abilities to help further your ambitions. Your reputation may be enhanced by group interactions, auditions, and public appearances. Express yourself artistically, using your imagination, intuition, and inspiration for artistic creation.

### November Vibrations (8 PY)

This month will be active, full of new people, situations, and ideas. This is definitely a time to start a new activity, friendship, or vocation. Take advantage of a change that comes into effect. Changes will bring new solutions to some old problems. Take the initiative to move yourself forward because the ball's in your court. You'll be put in the driver's seat. It's up to you to act. Take a chance if the odds are in your favor, but realize that some of the things you begin will likely end next year. Be yourself and emphasize your abilities. Use originality and creativity, but don't go overboard and irritate or alienate others.

This month things get accomplished that were on the brink of completion three months ago but didn't materialize. Financial benefits, recognition and publicity are rewards for your hard work. Be aggressive and make changes, breaking up old conditions you don't like and strengthening weak areas. Look for something meaningful. Base your decisions on independent and intellectual evaluations because you probably won't get any help or encouragement from others.

You may come to the realization that some of your current ventures will change or be phased out during the coming year. Realize that you will probably be heading in a completely different direction next year. Although this may have you concerned or worried, it's important to remember that life is change and growth is optional. You must choose your path wisely.

## December Vibrations (8 PY)

This month offers an opportunity for you to interact with friends and lovers and to make others happy. Although you feel the urge to act, this isn't the time to be ambitious or to make any material changes. Instead, this is a time for you to work quietly, to take care of the details that may slow you down later. Wait patiently for developments, even though it may seem as though nothing is happening.

Rest and allow friends, lovers, and business associates time to think and adjust to things that may differ from their personal desires. At times, situations arise that require you to be diplomatic, considerate, and tactful. Help resolve family squabbles or quarrels by using your sensitivity and tactful approach. Don't force issues. You may have to compromise and back down on a threat. Do the little things that you overlooked last month. Use this month to cooperate with others while working on your projects, or help others with their ventures.

Discuss your future plans with friends who may be able to suggest some educational pursuits which could prove to be useful to you when next year rolls around. Be open-minded as you listen to others' sly remarks or constructive criticisms that may prove to be helpful. You may be overly sensitive and self-conscious, taking what others say the "wrong way" and end up with hurt feelings. Don't be that way. Try to be adaptable, understanding, and courteous.

Participate in family festivities and social gatherings. Renew some of your friendships, visit old friends you haven't seen in awhile. It will be very important for you to take special time for loved ones; spend enjoyable activities with children and close friends or relatives. Reflect on the past year and pay attention to the things you've learned.

# 9 PERSONAL YEAR VIBRATION

This year will bring many of your affairs to a head. You will see the completion and fulfillment of some of your dreams. This is not the best time to enter into a new business, marriage, new jobs, or partnerships. It is, however, the best time to sort through your life, recognize immature emotions, negative thinking, restrictive behavior patterns, and get rid of them. This is the year to throw out old clothes, let go of lost loves, and reread good books. Clinging to the past will only cause problems for the future. What appears to be a loss will actually turn out to be a better way in the end. It's time to let go, now.

If possible, don't start anything new or make major decisions, especially something major like marriage or a new business, until after September. Better yet, wait until next year. Exercise caution in all major decisions. If you plan on cementing a personal relationship, consider your motives for marriage very carefully. Even if you and your significant other have been together for years, this is not the year to get married. Pay heed to this warning. Personal relationships or business activities started during this year could end prematurely.

You will experience mood swings and unexpected happenings. Life will bring you events of significance filled with much confusion and feeling. Floundering friendships, marriages, and partnerships will have to be faced and dealt with. Endings usually indicate a change of interests or moving apart from a close relationship. You must be willing to let go of relationships that are no longer in touch with the changes taking place in your life. If something asks for freedom, it's important for you to let go because if you try to hold on, it may get away anyway. Experiences or relationships that go out of your life can leave a deep feeling of loss and open old wounds. Don't continue a relationship you want ended just because emotions are high. It's time to carry forward only those relationships and experiences with promise, and let new contacts and acquaintances in to add vitality and positive development to your life.

Don't look at the completion as a failure or sorrow. Instead, it's really a reward, for through completion you can open the way to new opportunities and new interests. Even though it may not be apparent right away, understand that endings allow more freedom. Your use of clear thought and action will probably be impeded because your emotions are extremely active and difficult to deal with. By year's end you will realize that old habits or characteristics that you thought were essential to your identity will no longer be valid. If you are tolerant, compassionate, and forgiving, then this can and will be one of the most wonderful years of your life.

This year love will be offered but will be from impersonal admirers and of short duration. Love affairs through personal vanity will easily break up. You will find love affairs interesting, both yours and others, and you may be called to help straighten out another's problems. You will find rewards through what you do for others.

Love will be disturbing if too personal or clinging. You may have to learn the lesson that ultimate love doesn't restrict or bind, but rather supports freedom. In fact, quite possibly a deep and lasting love will have to be given up to teach you the lesson of understanding that true love simply loves and doesn't seek to hold or limit.

Trying to rekindle old flames will cause your emotions to swing from one extreme to the other. Instead of instigating or legalizing ideas or affiliations, be patient. This year, be a rolling stone gathering no moss. Comfortable habits, whether they are pleasant or not, will be difficult to let go. Realize that changes are necessary and some things must be terminated. Something better is just around the corner.

Things that occurred during the past eight years will reappear. You may return to your old neighborhood, try on clothes that were carefully packed away in the attic, or ask for dinners like your mother used to make. You'll have to develop a sense of calmness, balance, and an acceptance of life. Once you learn to let go you will be able to receive.

If your marriage was rocky or close to an end two years ago, this year the divorce will become final. Deep feelings will have to be worked through. Forgive those in your past and let them get on with their lives, just as you must get on with yours. If you hang on to negative attachments through anger or a sense that justice hasn't been served, you'll only bring misery to yourself. Selfishness, negativity, anger and pettiness will only blow up in your face. It's time to forgive, let go and move on.

You may be involved in legal struggles with large corporations. If you are right, put up a good fight, with tolerance and compassion as part of your effort. Lawsuits happen when there is a lack of honesty and others may try to take what is not rightfully theirs. Quarrels will gain very little and legal matters can be long drawn out battles. Egotism and a strong need for popularity without good works will end in loss and regret. Honesty is the best policy at all times and will bring you the assistance you need to win. At times you might feel like giving in, or giving up, but if you sacrifice your principles you'll end up disappointed in the end. It's important for you to stay true to yourself.

A dominant character may be in your life (business or personal) causing you unhappiness, leading to sorrow and separations. It may seem as though others are at fault and causing you problems. This feeling is probably exaggerated by your heightened sensitivity and volatile emotional moods. Control your mood swings, don't allow yourself to slip into feelings of self-pity and insecurity. Watch for feelings of resentment and jealousy or you may lose opportunities. Don't play the blame game. Take back your power.

This year demands a strong character and high principles, bringing with it many experiences and emotional tests, both disappointing and rewarding. If you're not careful, nervous strain and worry can cause health problems. Remind yourself now and then that when you worry you're paying interest on something that hasn't happened yet. Keep physically fit and exercise if you can. Be careful and watch what you do as you could be more accident-prone during the year.

Travel if you can. In fact, traveling a long-distance, visiting neighboring countries, or overseas is possible. Get out and smell the roses, feel the breeze, listen to the birds, or reminisce with old friends. If you are involved in the arts, either as an actor, writer, or performer, you'll see an enhancement of your talents and the opening up of many new opportunities for your advancement and growth. Listen to your intuition. This is a time for self-investigation and cleansing. Learn to be alone. In this friendship year, express love and affection to the many and tolerance to all.

If possible, pay up all debts in full before the new year begins. If you don't start fresh next year, you will be hampered by old relationships, obligations or business. Try to give some thought to areas for development when next year begins. Money and the best things life has to offer can be made and retained, but just as easily lost, only to be made again. This year seeks to reward your efforts with the best life has to offer—love, attainment, financial improvement—as long as you think and act with more love, tolerance, and compassion. Sensitivity and working for the good of humanity will bring you success.

### Personal Month Vibrations in a 9 Personal Year
The following is a brief outline of the vibrations you can expect during the 9 Personal

Year (for a more detailed description of what a specific month has in store for you, read the information found under the month heading, at the end of this section).

The year starts off with a feeling of extra power. Change is in the air, but don't expect plans made now to last beyond the year. Get a new viewpoint of an old project or find a way to accomplish the final stages.

During February be careful not to give in to low spirits or fatigue. Watch your health; this would be a good time for you to get a major checkup. Think twice, then think again before getting married. A relationship may end now; if you need to, talk to someone about your feelings.

March brings situations requiring you to have an attractive appearance and to put on a happy face. Have fun with friends and lovers.

Use April to reconstruct plans or projects and take care of any mistakes in finance or judgment. Situations will arise that demand a straightforward approach.

In the spring, you could receive recognition for creative efforts. Look at past accomplishments and prepare to begin new long-term goals. Take one last long look at old flames, school chums, or personal ideals. Do what you feel is necessary. Keep busy and accept new opportunities if they come to you, but you may not see the way clearly until after September.

During May you could be involved in heavy sexual or romantic interludes which may prove to be a flash in the pan. You may experience a conflict between the desire to expand and a desire to complete. Be venturesome and try something different, spontaneous, and dress to attract attention.

In June, you may suffer the loss of a business or personal relationship. Endings related to love and romance are likely to be extremely emotional. An inheritance or monetary gift could give you a feeling of security.

If possible, take a vacation in July, or at least take some time to yourself and do the things you've been wanting to do. Take steps to finish a project or let it end of its own accord.

The summer months bring feelings of loneliness. In August, apply yourself to complete a project. If you take advantage of endings, opportunities for advancement, recognition, financial improvement, and business expansion will be there, but only if you are organized, tactful and persuasive. Work with international agencies, large corporations or charities, publishing, research, or pursue worthwhile cultural projects. Exceptional results will be achieved, although the results will not be seen until September or October.

At times during the summer months, you may feel held back, unable to keep things moving steadily forward. You will be required to make a major life decision and must use sound judgment. Meditate and pray for answers or guidance.

September brings feelings of disillusionment and disappointment as a result of summer's romantic and misunderstood ideas. It's time to tie up loose ends. Try to be cooperative and generous in thoughts and feelings. Watch for volatile emotions. If something goes out of your life, let it go. Endings clear the way for future happiness and good.

October brings new ideas that will probably be of short duration. You may change jobs or move if you feel you have to. Sort out priorities and plan, but it's best to wait until next April. Instead, spend time working to improve relationships, entertain and inspire others.

November brings petty annoyances and emotional irritants. Intimate relationships will flourish if you are open to follow the other's lead. Wait for developments and see how your ideas of last month are working out. Send a card to someone special, send flowers to a friend, do the little things that you overlooked last month.

In December, reminisce over the good memories of the past nine years and look ahead. Things that were working underneath the surface will come to light. Expect all talk and no action until December 31st, when an unconventional and surprising observation will decide the most important finalization of the year. Something or someone will alter the course of next year's independent goals.

## January Vibrations (9 PY)

This month will be active, full of new people, situations, and ideas. This is definitely a time to start a new activity, friendship, vocation, or hobby. A change may come into effect, bringing new solutions to some old problems, take the initiative to move yourself forward.

There may be a number of new and promising enterprises that come your way. Since this is a year of endings, take special care that you are not taken in by smooth talkers. No matter how good the potential looks, a new venture will complete itself by August of the following year. However, a new opportunity may help you to close or phase out some of your previous, long-term endeavors. It will be up to you to decide what you should do.

This month things get accomplished that were on the brink of completion three months ago but didn't materialize. Be aggressive and make changes. Break up old conditions you don't like and strengthen weak areas. Base your decisions on independent and intellectual evaluations because you probably won't get any help or encouragement from others.

You'll get the feeling that there's something out there that you need to do, but what? This year finding the correct direction or action to take will be difficult as things seem so uncertain at the moment.

Take a chance if the odds are in your favor. Be yourself and emphasize your abilities. Use originality and creativity, but don't go overboard and irritate or alienate others. Act with sensitivity and try to understand your friends and family.

### February Vibrations (9 PY)

Although your parents or friends feel this is a good time for you to finally bite the bullet and get married, don't. If you've waited this long to tie the knot, wait another year or at least until after September. If you don't heed the warning, expect trouble in the relationship, with things coming to a head in a few months, or the marriage ending in divorce or separation by August of the following year.

This month offers an opportunity for you to interact with friends and lovers and to make others happy. Although you feel the urge to act, this isn't the time to be ambitious or to make any material changes. Instead, this is a time for you to work quietly, to take care of the details that may slow you down later. Wait patiently for developments, even though it may seem as though nothing is happening.

Rest and allow friends, lovers, and business associates time to think and adjust to things that may differ from their personal desires. At times, situations arise that require you to be diplomatic, considerate, and tactful. Don't force issues. Instead, be supportive and sensitive to the feelings of others, especially if they become uneasy or edgy. Reassure your loved ones that you care for them if they question you. Show more love, affection, and caring to those closest to your heart. Acting with understanding should help smooth over disagreements.

You may begin to feel or see signs of the endings that are coming around the corner. Take time to think and realize that whatever happens is beyond your control. You may have to compromise and do the little things that you overlooked last month. Use this month to cooperate with others while working on your projects, or help others with their ventures.

Be open-minded as you listen to others' sly remarks or constructive criticisms that may prove to be helpful. You may be overly sensitive and self-conscious, taking what others say the "wrong way" and end up with hurt feelings. Don't be that way. Try to be adaptable, understanding, and courteous while you wait for developments.

## March Vibrations (9 PY)

This is a good month to take a short vacation or a long-distance trip if it's within your budget. You will have an opportunity to feel happy, cheerful, playful, and self-expressive. This is a month to enjoy friends, to entertain and be entertained. There will be may parties or social functions to attend, and energetic people to meet. The friends you meet may open doors to new opportunities.

Situations will arise requiring you to have an attractive appearance and to put on a happy face. Call old friends you haven't talked to in awhile; take a phone number at a party and make a new contact. Remaining sensitive to others' feelings may be difficult and you will be required to exercise self-control when using words. Close friends may cause you some emotional disturbances through their carelessness or insensitivity. Unless you handle your emotions with kid gloves, problems could arise and eventually lead to the termination of a friendship you've had for many years. It may become clear to you that a parting of the ways is inevitable. Accept what may happen without trying to hold on.

Shop for new clothes or decorate your home, but expect to lose money through frivolousness and extravagance. If you can leave the house without it, leave your credit card behind.

The projects you began four months ago will start to bloom. Use this month to talk about your ideas, show off your talents, and have fun with friends, lovers, and coworkers. All forms of communication will be important. Express yourself, use imagination, intuition, and inspiration in creative activities. Write, dance, paint, cook, or play a musical instrument. Just be creative and have fun!

## April Vibrations (9 PY)

At the beginning of the month there may still be some social activity left over from last month. Enjoy yourself, but this is not the time to party. Instead, this is a month to work. Through hard work you'll have an opportunity to produce substantial results. Use your organizational abilities to move a project or business venture toward closure. You must seriously apply yourself with regard to money, routines, and physical fitness.

This month isn't the time to be lazy, disorganized, or impractical. Instead, you must use this month to reconstruct plans or projects and take care of any mistakes in finance or judgment. Put everything in order to get ventures under way.

There may be a new opportunity or endeavor that comes your way and you may be interested in pursuing it. Situations will arise that demand a straightforward approach. Face facts; research your ideas and don't gamble on the unknown. Maybe now is a good time for you to realize that some of your old ways of being and doing just aren't right for you anymore.

At times, you'll probably feel limited or restricted. It's important that you take time to analyze the limitations or restrictions and see whether they are of your own making. If so, plan to eliminate them. You might have to change your point of view. An "attitude adjustment" could be in store. Some limitations are unchangeable and you'll have to learn how to deal with them in a more satisfactory manner.

Take on more domestic responsibility with a smile on your face. Work instead of talking about what needs to be done. Be efficient and stabilize your finances. Follow through on commitments, organize time, and above all don't waste your energy. You may feel a bit stressed, so remember to take care of your health. This is a time to throw silly notions out the window and be practical.

## May Vibrations (9 PY)

This month offers you an opportunity to expand your horizons, to progress, and make changes. You should get out and meet new people, see new places, experience new activities, and have unusual opportunities. The new friends you meet may open doors to future endeavors.

Try to minimize responsibilities if you can, but don't ignore them. Watch legal commitments and expect conflicts and outbursts. It may take an extra effort on your part so things don't get out of hand. Take a chance on luck and love, although love affairs may not last. It is wise not to spend too much of your time on frivolous pursuits.

Situations will arise requiring you to follow a hunch. Study and research the possibilities. If the odds are in your favor take a chance, but only if it's worth your while. Business ventures or prospects might look tempting, especially if a good presenter has you enticed. Watch that you aren't fooled. Things that are worthwhile take time to grow. Look into beginning things in the future, say six months down the road. Whimsical ideas, travel, and a drive toward less responsibility are in the air. In fact, if you travel, you may find unusual or unexpected possibilities.

Try something different, spontaneous, dress to attract attention, and exercise. Drop the old and look for the new. Be careful not to run yourself ragged. Don't lack focus, becoming unreliable, temperamental, and frustrated. Unexpected possibilities are around every corner, so be flexible, broad-minded, and full of energy.

## June Vibrations (9 PY)

This month gives you an opportunity to pay attention to loved ones and home or community duties and responsibilities. This is your domestic month. Don't travel unless you're going to visit family. Be sure to maintain peaceful relationships, make domestic improvements, and be emotionally responsive. The time is right to settle down, deepen love, and create harmony. You can enjoy sharing chores and good times with family or friends. Take time to enjoy children and to participate in children's activities.

This is a good time to enjoy the pleasures of romance and love. Keep your emotions in balance and show a great deal of affection. In fact, the more love you give, the more you will receive. At times, situations will arise that require you to sacrifice some of your personal desires. Use this month to be of service. Give of yourself taking time to teach, pacify, and indicate approval. Through serving others you may find doors opening to new opportunities.

Be mature, devoted, and trustworthy when dealing with emotions. Don't be stubborn, intolerant, or worrying. A close friendship may be coming to a parting of ways. Disagreements from the past that weren't resolved, won't be resolved now and you should accept the ending. Some endings are unpreventable, no matter how hard you try to hang on, and you'll have to deal with strong emotions and much drama. Try to keep things on an even keel and balanced as you say goodbye. Help others do the same, regardless of the feelings being displayed. If you take time to analyze things, you might be able to see that although you don't want this friendship to end, you'll have much more freedom once it's gone.

People come and go throughout our lives. They bring with them special talents and abilities that help us (and vice-versa) on our journey through life. Once their time is served, and we outgrow the association, it's time to make room for new friendships.

Use your imagination and express yourself artistically. Write, paint, cook, or play a musical instrument. The focus on this month is to provide a peaceful, happy, peaceful, and beautiful environment in your home.

## July Vibrations (9 PY)

This month gives you an opportunity to spend time alone, to analyze and clarify your goals, to learn from the past, and to plan for the future. You may enlist the aid of professionals (lawyers, therapists, counselors) or look into religious or metaphysical studies. You'll seem to be drawn to the unusual. You may learn something of significance for the future.

Instead of taking action this month, wait and analyze current legal dealings, questionable relationships, and future plans or goals. You should have a broad-minded, analytical, and critical point of view. But watch that you don't become too intellectual, thinking only from your mind, remember to use your heart, too.

This isn't the month to be aggressive, sociable, or to pursue commercial ambitions. Think before speaking and examine the opinions of others carefully. Don't take what others say as gospel unless you are sure. Be a little secretive; don't reveal your thoughts.

Now is the time to think about positive endings to situations or relationships that have hampered you in the past. Take stock of the people and activities that have held you back. If you notice someone is drifting away, let them go. Avoid quarrelling and harsh words. The pen is mightier than the sword, so watch the words your write as they could cause problems. Realize that although you may have tried to discuss things clearly, misunderstandings happen and others may not be willing to drop the argument.

Take time to be alone, read, study, research, write, teach, or enjoy philosophical conversations. Wait for the telephone to ring instead of being the one to call. This month you must be patient, tolerant, and willing to spend time alone. If possible, spend some time in the country, take a short vacation, or change your diet and exercise. Go for long walks. If possible, make time for a dental or physical checkup.

## August Vibrations (9 PY)

This month gives you an opportunity to take control of business and financial matters. You should rely on yourself, be forceful, self-confident, act decisively, approach matters in a businesslike manner, dress with dignity, and express yourself with authority. You will have more ability to make things happen with regard to business or financial matters than in any other month. This isn't the time for vacations or undisciplined behavior. Be sensitive, tactful, and compassionate when dealing with coworkers.

You'll have to make a major decision involving money. It will be important for you not to procrastinate. Opportunities for advancement, recognition, financial improvement, and business expansion are there, but only happen if you are organized, tactful, and persuasive. Associate with high-powered and enterprising people to help you take advantage of the opportunities. New interests may have significant potential for future development and financial benefits. Be on the lookout for the possibilities and watch that associates don't sneak things past you or try to hide things that might be of benefit to you. Take a helping hand if it's offered.

If you advertise and promote the projects you started eight or nine years ago, exceptional results will be achieved. Hard work and long hours may strain personal relationships.

## September Vibrations (9 PY)

This month gives you an opportunity to complete projects, be charitable, tolerant, and compassionate. Use this time to help others, to be generous, kind, and inspire or counsel those who are in need of your support. Try to give of yourself with little thought of reward. At times, situations will arise requiring you to have an unselfish, broad-minded attitude. Give blood, visit the elderly, needy, or sick and take a book, a treat, or a listening ear.

The projects, activities, or relationships that began eight or nine years ago are either completed or abandoned, causing you to readjust to different circumstances. The endings will likely be connected to much drama and strong emotions. Try to be understanding and compassionate regardless of the situation. This isn't the time to begin anything new or to force your will on others.

Know that the door is slowly opening up to a new future. Drama and confused feelings will be prevalent during this month. It's hard to finally say goodbye to old friends or relationships that have been comfortable until now. Try to keep emotions intact, exercising restraint when arguments erupt or people want to start a quarrel with you.

Some endings may be initiated by you as you begin to realize certain relationships are just draining you mentally with their negativity and self-absorbed lives. You may come to a realization that those people you considered friends really weren't. You'll be surprised to find that when you really pay attention to your thoughts, you don't miss those negative relationships and are actually looking forward to a time without them.

Take a long-distance trip if it's within your budget. This month can be used to meet with notable or helpful people who have the contacts or abilities to help further your ambitions. Your reputation may be enhanced by group interactions, auditions, and public appearances. Express yourself artistically, using your imagination, intuition, and inspiration for artistic creation. Finally take the time to finish that manuscript or painting. Write, paint, sing, dance, play a musical instrument, or learn to cook a new dish. Do something creative to take your mind off the endings for awhile.

## October Vibrations (9 PY)

This month will be active, full of new people, situations, and ideas. You'll feel upbeat and ready for something to begin. This is definitely a time to start a new activity, friendship, or vocation. A change may come into effect, bringing new solutions to some old problems, take the initiative to move yourself forward. You'll be put in the driver's seat. It's up to you to act on the new ventures or opportunities that begin to open up.

This month things get accomplished that were on the brink of completion three months ago but didn't materialize. Be aggressive and make changes. Break up old conditions you don't like and strengthen weak areas. Base your decisions on independent and intellectual evaluations because you probably won't get any help or encouragement from others. You may feel differently about yourself and your situation. The future looks exciting and new and you almost can't wait for next year to arrive.

Take a chance if the odds are in your favor. Be yourself and emphasize your abilities. Use originality and creativity, but don't go overboard and irritate or alienate others. Always keep in mind that others have feelings and thoughts that matter, too.

## November Vibrations (9 PY)
This month offers an opportunity for you to interact with friends and lovers and to make others happy. Although you feel the urge to act, this isn't the time to be ambitious or to make any material changes. Instead, this is a time for you to work quietly, to take care of the details that may slow you down later. Wait patiently for developments, even though you're raring to go and it seems as though nothing is happening. Patience is a virtue that you need right now. Otherwise, if you push or try to force projects to move along quicker, you may hamper your possibilities for success in the future.

Rest and allow friends, lovers, and business associates time to think and adjust to things that may differ from their personal desires. At times, situations arise that require you to be diplomatic, considerate, and tactful. Don't force issues. You may have to compromise and do the little things that you overlooked last month. Use this month to cooperate with others while working on your projects, or help others with their ventures.

Be open-minded as you listen to others' sly remarks or constructive criticisms that may prove to be helpful. You may be overly sensitive and self-conscious, taking what others say the "wrong way" and end up with hurt feelings. Don't be that way. Try to be adaptable, understanding, and courteous while you wait (patiently) for developments.

### December Vibrations (9 PY)

During this festive month you will have an opportunity to feel happy, cheerful, playful, and self-expressive. This is a month to enjoy friends, to entertain and be entertained. You'll have an active social life. There will be many parties or social functions to attend, and energetic people to meet. Enjoy those you hold close to your heart. In fact, why don't you throw a party? Look for ways to have fun with friends, relatives, and children.

Situations will arise requiring you to have an attractive appearance and to put on a happy face. This is a good month to take a short vacation or to travel. Shop for new clothes or decorate your home, but expect to lose money through frivolousness and extravagance. It's best to leave your credit card behind.

Call old friends you haven't talked to in awhile; take a phone number at a party and make a new contact. The friends you meet may open doors to new opportunities. Use this month to talk about your ideas, show off your talents, and have fun with friends, lovers, and coworkers.

The projects you began four months ago will start to bloom. All forms of communication will be important. Express yourself, use imagination, intuition, and inspiration in creative activities. Write, dance, paint, cook, or play a musical instrument. Just be creative and have fun!

# PERSONAL DAY VIBRATIONS

The personal day has its own vibrations and can assist you in your daily routine, for guidance, making plans and decisions, and taking advantage of opportunities at the right time.

Reading what your personal day has in store for you can prove to be quite helpful. Many personal problems can be solved by wisely using the instructions. Help romance by looking up your partner's personal day vibration and you might just be able to figure out what kind of mood he's in or why she's acting a certain way. You'll understand why some days are better for business than others. You can see why certain things take place, why events scheduled are delayed, or why the unexpected happens on certain days.

Some days have stronger, negative vibrations that must be overcome in order for you to reach the positive aspects of the day. These days are: 13/4, 14/5, 16/7, and 19/1. Days that you may feel more nervous tension than normal are: 11/2 and 22/4.

There really are no bad days. It all depends on how you handle the experience and your attitude at the time. You must remember: Your life depends on what you choose to do in the circumstances in which you find yourself.

Refer to the charts on the following pages to find your personal day number. Choose the chart for your current personal year, then pick the date you want to know about. The descriptions for each personal day begin on page 136.

## Personal Days in a 1 Personal Year Vibration:

| DATES | JAN | FEB | MAR | APR | MAY | JUN |
|---|---|---|---|---|---|---|
| 1, 10, 19, 28, | 3 | 4 | 5 | 6 | 7 | 8 |
| 2, 20 | 4 | 5 | 6 | 7 | 8 | 9 |
| 11, 29 | 13/4 | 14/5 | 6 | 16/7 | 8 | 9 |
| 3, 12, 21, 30 | 5 | 6 | 7 | 8 | 9 | 1 |
| 4, 13, 22, 31 | 6 | 7 | 8 | 9 | 1 | 11/2 |
| 5, 14, 23 | 7 | 8 | 9 | 1 | 11/2 | 3 |
| 6, 15, 24 | 8 | 9 | 1 | 11/2 | 3 | 13/4 |
| 7, 16, 25 | 9 | 1 | 11/2 | 3 | 13/4 | 14/5 |
| 8, 17, 26 | 1 | 11/2 | 3 | 13/4 | 14/5 | 6 |
| 9, 18, 27 | 11/2 | 3 | 13/4 | 14/5 | 6 | 16/7 |

| DATES | JUL | AUG | SEPT | OCT | NOV | DEC |
|---|---|---|---|---|---|---|
| 1, 10, 19, 28, | 9 | 1 | 11/2 | 3 | 13/4 | 5 |
| 2, 20 | 1 | 11/2 | 3 | 4 | 14/5 | 6 |
| 11, 29 | 19/1 | 2 | 3 | 13/4 | 5 | 6 |
| 3, 12, 21, 30 | 11/2 | 3 | 13/4 | 5 | 6 | 7 |
| 4, 13, 22, 31 | 3 | 13/4 | 14/5 | 6 | 16/7 | 8 |
| 5, 14, 23 | 13/4 | 14/5 | 6 | 7 | 8 | 9 |
| 6, 15, 24 | 14/5 | 6 | 16/7 | 8 | 9 | 1 |
| 7, 16, 25 | 6 | 16/7 | 8 | 9 | 19/1 | 11/2 |
| 8, 17, 26 | 16/7 | 8 | 9 | 1 | 2 | 3 |
| 9, 18, 27 | 8 | 9 | 19/1 | 11/2 | 3 | 13/4 |

# PERSONAL DAY VIBRATIONS

*Personal Days in a 2 Personal Year Vibration:*

| DATES | JAN | FEB | MAR | APR | MAY | JUN |
|---|---|---|---|---|---|---|
| 1, 10, 19, 28, | 4 | 5 | 6 | 7 | 8 | 9 |
| 2, 20 | 5 | 6 | 7 | 8 | 9 | 1 |
| 11, 29 | 14/5 | 6 | 16/7 | 8 | 9 | 19/1 |
| 3, 12, 21, 30 | 6 | 7 | 8 | 9 | 1 | 11/2 |
| 4, 13, 22, 31 | 7 | 8 | 9 | 1 | 11/2 | 3 |
| 5, 14, 23 | 8 | 9 | 1 | 11/2 | 3 | 13/4 |
| 6, 15, 24 | 9 | 1 | 11/2 | 3 | 13/4 | 14/5 |
| 7, 16, 25 | 1 | 11/2 | 3 | 13/4 | 14/5 | 6 |
| 8, 17, 26 | 11/2 | 3 | 13/4 | 14/5 | 6 | 16/7 |
| 9, 18, 27 | 3 | 13/4 | 14/5 | 6 | 16/7 | 8 |

| DATES | JUL | AUG | SEPT | OCT | NOV | DEC |
|---|---|---|---|---|---|---|
| 1, 10, 19, 28, | 1 | 11/2 | 3 | 4 | 14/5 | 6 |
| 2, 20 | 11/2 | 3 | 13/4 | 5 | 6 | 7 |
| 11, 29 | 2 | 3 | 22/4 | 14/5 | 6 | 16/7 |
| 3, 12, 21, 30 | 3 | 13/4 | 14/5 | 6 | 16/7 | 8 |
| 4, 13, 22, 31 | 13/4 | 14/5 | 6 | 7 | 8 | 9 |
| 5, 14, 23 | 14/5 | 6 | 16/7 | 8 | 9 | 1 |
| 6, 15, 24 | 6 | 16/7 | 8 | 9 | 19/1 | 11/2 |
| 7, 16, 25 | 16/7 | 8 | 9 | 1 | 2 | 3 |
| 8, 17, 26 | 8 | 9 | 19/1 | 11/2 | 3 | 13/4 |
| 9, 18, 27 | 9 | 19/1 | 2 | 3 | 22/4 | 14/5 |

PERSONAL DAY VIBRATIONS

*Personal Days in a 3 Personal Year Vibration:*

| DATES | JAN | FEB | MAR | APR | MAY | JUN |
|---|---|---|---|---|---|---|
| 1, 10, 19, 28, | 5 | 6 | 7 | 8 | 9 | 1 |
| 2, 20 | 6 | 7 | 8 | 9 | 1 | 11/2 |
| 11, 29 | 6 | 16/7 | 8 | 9 | 19/1 | 2 |
| 3, 12, 21, 30 | 7 | 8 | 9 | 1 | 11/2 | 3 |
| 4, 13, 22, 31 | 8 | 9 | 1 | 11/2 | 3 | 13/4 |
| 5, 14, 23 | 9 | 1 | 11/2 | 3 | 13/4 | 14/5 |
| 6, 15, 24 | 1 | 11/2 | 3 | 13/4 | 14/5 | 6 |
| 7, 16, 25 | 11/2 | 3 | 13/4 | 14/5 | 6 | 16/7 |
| 8, 17, 26 | 3 | 13/4 | 14/5 | 6 | 16/7 | 8 |
| 9, 18, 27 | 13/4 | 14/5 | 6 | 16/7 | 8 | 9 |

| DATES | JUL | AUG | SEPT | OCT | NOV | DEC |
|---|---|---|---|---|---|---|
| 1, 10, 19, 28, | 11/2 | 3 | 13/4 | 5 | 6 | 7 |
| 2, 20 | 2 | 3 | 14/5 | 6 | 16/7 | 8 |
| 11, 29 | 3 | 13/4 | 5 | 6 | 7 | 8 |
| 3, 12, 21, 30 | 13/4 | 14/5 | 6 | 7 | 8 | 9 |
| 4, 13, 22, 31 | 14/5 | 6 | 16/7 | 8 | 9 | 1 |
| 5, 14, 23 | 6 | 16/7 | 8 | 9 | 19/1 | 11/2 |
| 6, 15, 24 | 16/7 | 8 | 9 | 1 | 2 | 3 |
| 7, 16, 25 | 8 | 9 | 19/1 | 11/2 | 3 | 13/4 |
| 8, 17, 26 | 9 | 19/1 | 2 | 3 | 22/4 | 14/5 |
| 9, 18, 27 | 19/1 | 2 | 3 | 13/4 | 5 | 6 |

*Personal Days in a 4 Personal Year Vibration:*

| DATES | JAN | FEB | MAR | APR | MAY | JUN |
|-------|-----|-----|-----|-----|-----|-----|
| 1, 10, 19, 28, | 6 | 7 | 8 | 9 | 1 | 11/2 |
| 2, 20 | 7 | 8 | 9 | 1 | 11/2 | 3 |
| 11, 29 | 16/7 | 8 | 9 | 19/1 | 2 | 3 |
| 3, 12, 21, 30 | 8 | 9 | 1 | 11/2 | 3 | 13/4 |
| 4, 13, 22, 31 | 9 | 1 | 11/2 | 3 | 13/4 | 14/5 |
| 5, 14, 23 | 1 | 11/2 | 3 | 13/4 | 14/5 | 6 |
| 6, 15, 24 | 11/2 | 3 | 13/4 | 14/5 | 6 | 16/7 |
| 7, 16, 25 | 3 | 13/4 | 14/5 | 6 | 16/7 | 8 |
| 8, 17, 26 | 13/4 | 14/5 | 6 | 16/7 | 8 | 9 |
| 9, 18, 27 | 14/5 | 6 | 16/7 | 8 | 9 | 19/1 |

| DATES | JUL | AUG | SEPT | OCT | NOV | DEC |
|-------|-----|-----|------|-----|-----|-----|
| 1, 10, 19, 28, | 3 | 13/4 | 14/5 | 6 | 16/7 | 8 |
| 2, 20 | 13/4 | 14/5 | 6 | 7 | 8 | 9 |
| 11, 29 | 22/4 | 5 | 6 | 16/7 | 8 | 9 |
| 3, 12, 21, 30 | 14/5 | 6 | 16/7 | 8 | 9 | 1 |
| 4, 13, 22, 31 | 6 | 16/7 | 8 | 9 | 19/1 | 11/2 |
| 5, 14, 23 | 16/7 | 8 | 9 | 1 | 2 | 3 |
| 6, 15, 24 | 8 | 9 | 19/1 | 11/2 | 3 | 13/4 |
| 7, 16, 25 | 9 | 19/1 | 2 | 3 | 22/4 | 14/5 |
| 8, 17, 26 | 19/1 | 2 | 3 | 13/4 | 5 | 6 |
| 9, 18, 27 | 2 | 3 | 22/4 | 14/5 | 6 | 16/7 |

*Personal Days in a 5 Personal Year Vibration:*

| DATES | JAN | FEB | MAR | APR | MAY | JUN |
|---|---|---|---|---|---|---|
| 1, 10, 19, 28, | 7 | 8 | 9 | 1 | 11/2 | 3 |
| 2, 20 | 8 | 9 | 1 | 11/2 | 3 | 13/4 |
| 11, 29 | 8 | 9 | 19/1 | 2 | 3 | 22/4 |
| 3, 12, 21, 30 | 9 | 1 | 11/2 | 3 | 13/4 | 14/5 |
| 4, 13, 22, 31 | 1 | 11/2 | 3 | 13/4 | 14/5 | 6 |
| 5, 14, 23 | 11/2 | 3 | 13/4 | 14/5 | 6 | 16/7 |
| 6, 15, 24 | 3 | 13/4 | 14/5 | 6 | 16/7 | 8 |
| 7, 16, 25 | 13/4 | 14/5 | 6 | 16/7 | 8 | 9 |
| 8, 17, 26 | 14/5 | 6 | 16/7 | 8 | 9 | 19/1 |
| 9, 18, 27 | 6 | 16/7 | 8 | 9 | 19/1 | 2 |

| DATES | JUL | AUG | SEPT | OCT | NOV | DEC |
|---|---|---|---|---|---|---|
| 1, 10, 19, 28, | 13/4 | 14/5 | 6 | 7 | 8 | 9 |
| 2, 20 | 14/5 | 6 | 16/7 | 8 | 9 | 1 |
| 11, 29 | 5 | 6 | 7 | 8 | 9 | 19/1 |
| 3, 12, 21, 30 | 6 | 16/7 | 8 | 9 | 1 | 11/2 |
| 4, 13, 22, 31 | 16/7 | 8 | 9 | 1 | 2 | 3 |
| 5, 14, 23 | 8 | 9 | 19/1 | 11/2 | 3 | 13/4 |
| 6, 15, 24 | 9 | 19/1 | 2 | 3 | 22/4 | 14/5 |
| 7, 16, 25 | 19/1 | 2 | 3 | 13/4 | 5 | 6 |
| 8, 17, 26 | 2 | 3 | 22/4 | 14/5 | 6 | 16/7 |
| 9, 18, 27 | 3 | 22/4 | 5 | 6 | 7 | 8 |

*Personal Days in a 6 Personal Year Vibration:*

| DATES | JAN | FEB | MAR | APR | MAY | JUN |
|---|---|---|---|---|---|---|
| 1, 10, 19, 28, | 8 | 9 | 1 | 11/2 | 3 | 13/4 |
| 2, 20 | 9 | 1 | 11/2 | 3 | 13/4 | 14/5 |
| 11, 29 | 1 | 19/1 | 2 | 3 | 22/4 | 5 |
| 3, 12, 21, 30 | 1 | 11/2 | 3 | 13/4 | 14/5 | 6 |
| 4, 13, 22, 31 | 11/2 | 3 | 13/4 | 14/5 | 6 | 16/7 |
| 5, 14, 23 | 3 | 13/4 | 14/5 | 6 | 16/7 | 8 |
| 6, 15, 24 | 13/4 | 14/5 | 6 | 16/7 | 8 | 9 |
| 7, 16, 25 | 14/5 | 6 | 16/7 | 8 | 9 | 19/1 |
| 8, 17, 26 | 6 | 16/7 | 8 | 9 | 19/1 | 2 |
| 9, 18, 27 | 16/7 | 8 | 9 | 19/1 | 2 | 3 |

| DATES | JUL | AUG | SEPT | OCT | NOV | DEC |
|---|---|---|---|---|---|---|
| 1, 10, 19, 28, | 14/5 | 6 | 16/7 | 8 | 9 | 1 |
| 2, 20 | 6 | 16/7 | 8 | 9 | 19/1 | 11/2 |
| 11, 29 | 6 | 7 | 8 | 9 | 1 | 2 |
| 3, 12, 21, 30 | 16/7 | 8 | 9 | 1 | 2 | 3 |
| 4, 13, 22, 31 | 8 | 9 | 19/1 | 11/2 | 3 | 13/4 |
| 5, 14, 23 | 9 | 19/1 | 2 | 3 | 22/4 | 14/5 |
| 6, 15, 24 | 19/1 | 2 | 3 | 13/4 | 5 | 6 |
| 7, 16, 25 | 2 | 3 | 22/4 | 14/5 | 6 | 16/7 |
| 8, 17, 26 | 3 | 22/4 | 5 | 6 | 7 | 8 |
| 9, 18, 27 | 22/4 | 5 | 6 | 16/7 | 8 | 9 |

*Personal Days in a 7 Personal Year Vibration:*

| DATES | JAN | FEB | MAR | APR | MAY | JUN |
|---|---|---|---|---|---|---|
| 1, 10, 19, 28, | 9 | 1 | 11/2 | 3 | 13/4 | 14/5 |
| 2, 20 | 1 | 11/2 | 3 | 13/4 | 14/5 | 6 |
| 11, 29 | 19/1 | 2 | 3 | 22/4 | 5 | 6 |
| 3, 12, 21, 30 | 11/2 | 3 | 13/4 | 14/5 | 6 | 16/7 |
| 4, 13, 22, 31 | 3 | 13/4 | 14/5 | 6 | 16/7 | 8 |
| 5, 14, 23 | 13/4 | 14/5 | 6 | 16/7 | 8 | 9 |
| 6, 15, 24 | 14/5 | 6 | 16/7 | 8 | 9 | 19/1 |
| 7, 16, 25 | 6 | 16/7 | 8 | 9 | 19/1 | 2 |
| 8, 17, 26 | 16/7 | 8 | 9 | 19/1 | 2 | 3 |
| 9, 18, 27 | 8 | 9 | 19/1 | 2 | 3 | 22/4 |

| DATES | JUL | AUG | SEPT | OCT | NOV | DEC |
|---|---|---|---|---|---|---|
| 1, 10, 19, 28, | 6 | 16/7 | 8 | 9 | 19/1 | 11/2 |
| 2, 20 | 16/7 | 8 | 9 | 1 | 2 | 3 |
| 11, 29 | 7 | 8 | 9 | 19/1 | 11/2 | 3 |
| 3, 12, 21, 30 | 8 | 9 | 19/1 | 11/2 | 3 | 13/4 |
| 4, 13, 22, 31 | 9 | 19/1 | 2 | 3 | 22/4 | 14/5 |
| 5, 14, 23 | 19/1 | 2 | 3 | 13/4 | 5 | 6 |
| 6, 15, 24 | 2 | 3 | 22/4 | 14/5 | 6 | 16/7 |
| 7, 16, 25 | 3 | 22/4 | 5 | 6 | 7 | 8 |
| 8, 17, 26 | 22/4 | 5 | 6 | 16/7 | 8 | 9 |
| 9, 18, 27 | 5 | 6 | 7 | 8 | 9 | 19/1 |

*Personal Days in a 8 Personal Year Vibration:*

| DATES | JAN | FEB | MAR | APR | MAY | JUN |
|---|---|---|---|---|---|---|
| 1, 10, 19, 28, | 1 | 11/2 | 3 | 13/4 | 14/5 | 6 |
| 2, 20 | 11/2 | 3 | 13/4 | 14/5 | 6 | 16/7 |
| 11, 29 | 2 | 3 | 22/4 | 5 | 6 | 7 |
| 3, 12, 21, 30 | 3 | 13/4 | 14/5 | 6 | 16/7 | 8 |
| 4, 13, 22, 31 | 13/4 | 14/5 | 6 | 16/7 | 8 | 9 |
| 5, 14, 23 | 14/5 | 6 | 16/7 | 8 | 9 | 19/1 |
| 6, 15, 24 | 6 | 16/7 | 8 | 9 | 19/1 | 2 |
| 7, 16, 25 | 16/7 | 8 | 9 | 19/1 | 2 | 3 |
| 8, 17, 26 | 8 | 9 | 19/1 | 2 | 3 | 22/4 |
| 9, 18, 27 | 9 | 19/1 | 2 | 3 | 22/4 | 5 |

| DATES | JUL | AUG | SEPT | OCT | NOV | DEC |
|---|---|---|---|---|---|---|
| 1, 10, 19, 28, | 16/7 | 8 | 9 | 1 | 11/2 | 3 |
| 2, 20 | 8 | 9 | 19/1 | 11/2 | 3 | 13/4 |
| 11, 29 | 8 | 9 | 1 | 2 | 3 | 22/4 |
| 3, 12, 21, 30 | 9 | 19/1 | 2 | 3 | 13/4 | 14/5 |
| 4, 13, 22, 31 | 19/1 | 2 | 3 | 13/4 | 14/5 | 6 |
| 5, 14, 23 | 2 | 3 | 22/4 | 14/5 | 6 | 16/7 |
| 6, 15, 24 | 3 | 22/4 | 5 | 6 | 16/7 | 8 |
| 7, 16, 25 | 22/4 | 5 | 6 | 16/7 | 8 | 9 |
| 8, 17, 26 | 5 | 6 | 7 | 8 | 9 | 19/1 |
| 9, 18, 27 | 6 | 7 | 8 | 9 | 19/1 | 2 |

*Personal Days in a 9 Personal Year Vibration:*

| DATES | JAN | FEB | MAR | APR | MAY | JUN |
|---|---|---|---|---|---|---|
| 1, 10, 19, 28, | 11/2 | 3 | 13/4 | 14/5 | 6 | 16/7 |
| 2, 20 | 3 | 13/4 | 14/5 | 6 | 16/7 | 8 |
| 11, 29 | 3 | 22/4 | 5 | 6 | 7 | 8 |
| 3, 12, 21, 30 | 13/4 | 14/5 | 6 | 16/7 | 8 | 9 |
| 4, 13, 22, 31 | 14/5 | 6 | 16/7 | 8 | 9 | 19/1 |
| 5, 14, 23 | 6 | 16/7 | 8 | 9 | 19/1 | 2 |
| 6, 15, 24 | 16/7 | 8 | 9 | 19/1 | 2 | 3 |
| 7, 16, 25 | 8 | 9 | 19/1 | 2 | 3 | 22/4 |
| 8, 17, 26 | 9 | 19/1 | 2 | 3 | 22/4 | 5 |
| 9, 18, 27 | 19/1 | 2 | 3 | 22/4 | 5 | 6 |

| DATES | JUL | AUG | SEPT | OCT | NOV | DEC |
|---|---|---|---|---|---|---|
| 1, 10, 19, 28, | 8 | 9 | 19/1 | 11/2 | 3 | 13/4 |
| 2, 20 | 9 | 19/1 | 2 | 3 | 22/4 | 14/5 |
| 11, 29 | 9 | 1 | 11/2 | 3 | 4 | 5 |
| 3, 12, 21, 30 | 19/1 | 2 | 3 | 13/4 | 5 | 6 |
| 4, 13, 22, 31 | 2 | 3 | 22/4 | 14/5 | 6 | 16/7 |
| 5, 14, 23 | 3 | 22/4 | 5 | 6 | 7 | 8 |
| 6, 15, 24 | 22/4 | 5 | 6 | 16/7 | 8 | 9 |
| 7, 16, 25 | 5 | 6 | 7 | 8 | 9 | 19/1 |
| 8, 17, 26 | 6 | 7 | 8 | 9 | 1 | 2 |
| 9, 18, 27 | 7 | 8 | 9 | 19/1 | 11/2 | 3 |

# PERSONAL DAY VIBRATIONS

## 1 Personal Day Vibration

Action is the key word for today. You are likely to feel self-confident, energetic, independent, ambitious, and creative. Do something new. Don't waste one minute because this is a day full of opportunity and you might not get a second chance. Plan your personal commitments carefully and be sure to have a definite goal in sight. With courage, determination, and commitment you can carry out your plans to a successful completion.

Today you must be honest, have a positive attitude and face any problems that have been worrying you recently. Aim for the top and go after what you want. This is a great day for making major decisions, new moves and partnerships, starting a job, meeting a potential client, or taking a trip with a specific purpose. Use your intuition. You'll find your judgment is excellent. A clever new thought could open previously closed doors. Be aggressive and promote yourself and your ideas.

Today, the negative side of you might be prone to exhibiting the following traits: being too impulsive, unyielding, opinionated, demanding, confrontational, bossy, cynical, chauvinistic, indifferent, or procrastinating and lacking initiative. Watch for these behaviors, thoughts or feelings and work to overcome them. If you don't you may lose control of situations that are in your hands.

Wear something red to activate today's energetic and independent mood. This will be an active day and should definitely be used to begin something new.

## 2 Personal Day Vibration

This will be a day for thoughts and plans rather than for actions. Today, it's best to wake up with an easygoing attitude. Don't rush, show resentment, or take on major jobs. Stay at home if you can. Think over your problems and try to figure out the best way for you to solve them.

When involved with other people, use intuition and respond with sensitivity, but don't expose your own feelings to be hurt. Be kind, helpful, and understanding. Above all, try to keep things peaceful. Today, to avoid confrontations, you might have to be the one to "turn the other cheek."

Family, friends, and associates may want to do the talking, take the lead, or unload their assignments on you. It seems as though everyone is picking on you! Since nit-picking is in the air it may not be easy for you to keep calm, cool, and collected. Today, it's up to you to straighten out an argument or misunderstanding, apologize for your fault in it, after all it took two to start it.

This isn't the time to make waves or push for results. Sit back and let the phone ring because if you make the call, the person may not be there either physically or mentally. If you push, nothing will get accomplished and you'll end up becoming annoyed. Listen and think instead of talking too much. Incoming information will bring in benefits and, by becoming aware of subtle hints, you could learn something important for the future.

Collect anything you can: information, facts, new friends, or things. Don't enter into any form of agreement today, whether a verbal promise or a signed contract, the results will not be favorable.

Attend to personal details, avoid self-pity, and try to get things out of the way that could slow you down tomorrow. Don't attempt to alter plans or relationships; take whatever comes in today and have faith that future benefits will follow.

Today, the negative side of you might be prone to exhibiting the following traits: becoming a busybody or fault-finding, meddling, overly sensitive, timid, inconsiderate, tactless, unresponsive, careless, fearful, cowardly, and uncaring. Watch for these behaviors, thoughts or feelings and work to overcome them.

Wear yellow and seek the sunlight. Don't let the smile come off your face. The purpose of this day is to support yesterday's activities, gather information, cooperate with others, and quietly enjoy your own routine.

### 3 Personal Day Vibration

Today will be a particularly lucky day when you should get out and about, be seen and heard, and generally have a good time. There's plenty to be done, but you should have more than enough energy to cope with anything that comes your way today and still find time for fun.

Wake up with a happy, energetic, optimistic, and friendly attitude. Make this day cheerful and make someone smile. Give others the pleasure of your company, spread good news, tell a joke, and dress to attract attention. Pick up the phone and make time to listen and respond.

Refuse to talk about personal troubles and worries. Stay focused on the sunny side of life today. Listen to your dreams. Laugh at failures and try again. Remember that success is made up of a bunch of failures that finally worked.

Take whatever comes in with a grain of salt. Don't fall prey to negative thinking, worrying or gossiping. Watch that you don't scatter your energies or overindulge in food or drink. It's wise not to make commitments that will bind you or hold you down at a later date. Stay present in today, let tomorrow come tomorrow.

Today, the negative side of you might be prone to exhibiting the following traits:

moody, boastful, conceited, extravagant, irresponsible, lacking in concentration or direction, worrying, quarrelsome, self-indulgent, jealous, unfriendly, or unforgiving. Watch for these behaviors, thoughts or feelings and work to overcome them.

Use this day to visit friends, go see a movie, read a good book, play a musical instrument, write a poem, experiment with a new recipe, go shopping, play with children and pets, and enjoy a good laugh. Try to ease up on routines and material goals. Work may feel like play and there may be very little getting done. Wear orange and let the fun begin.

## 4 Personal Day Vibration

There won't be much excitement for you today as 4-days are always rather dull and routine, sometimes even boring. Try to wake up early, organize your plans with a determined attitude, and keep your nose to the grindstone.

Use patience and persevere to put your house, job, and social obligations in order. This is a good day to clean closets, weed the garden, mow the lawn, file important papers, or balance your checkbook. Make a personal commitment to stick with the job until it gets done. You just might end up with the satisfaction of getting those jobs out of the way that have been hanging around too long. Be practical, get all your chores done now so you will have more time to enjoy yourself tomorrow.

When dealing with superiors, maintain composure, be reasonable, frank and obedient. Correct mistakes and make improvements. Control impulses. Don't be innovative, lazy, changeable, or look for anything new. Taking the "easy way" doesn't always prove to be the best way in the long run.

Although you may feel creative, this isn't the time to experiment. You'll find that a new opportunity may be more difficult to deal with today than it would be tomorrow. Plans made today for tomorrow will likely be altered or canceled. This has proven true time and time again. If possible, plan future commitments or dates on another day.

Today, the negative side of you might be prone to exhibiting the following traits: argumentative, contradictory, headstrong, insensitive, opinionated, resistant, rigid, rude, stubborn, uncompromising, slipshod, unaccountable, unproductive, undecided, or narrow-minded. Watch for these behaviors, thoughts or feelings and work to overcome them.

Wear green today and get down to work. By the end of the day you'll have accomplished something.

## *5 Personal Day Vibration*

If you properly worked your 4-day yesterday, you owe yourself a vacation today. Wake up early or late and approach the day with an open mind. This will be a day to expect the unexpected because anything can happen and probably will.

Today will be full of excitement and adventure. Do the same things in a different way, experiment and change perspectives.

Take a long lunch if you can, dress to attract attention, be enthusiastic, and expect to be flexible. Be responsible when necessary, but let yourself feel restless, sexy, and sociable. Risks, freedom, and good times are around every corner. Be on the lookout for something to keep.

This is a good day for the spontaneous start of a trip or vacation. Make a blind date, take a prospective client to lunch, go to the racetrack, try something new, or do something on the spur of the moment. If there's something you've been wanting to do, something that's a little risky or scary, do it today. Your "luck" is with you and you should make the most of it.

The key for today is that you remain constructive and not destructive. Use good sense and don't allow your restlessness to lead you astray. Don't end up staring at the bottom of a vodka bottle, or taking your friend's girlfriend out to dinner, or betting on any old horse at the race track. Temptations of the flesh will be hard to resist, do the best you can. It would be wise to protect yourself sexually, and whatever you do, do not drink and drive.

Accidents can happen and in haste to get things done you may break a dish, cut yourself, or trip over your own feet. If your nerves get frayed, don't waste your vitality and energy in losing your temper, just be more careful and slow down.

Today, the negative side of you might be prone to exhibiting the following traits: impatient, agitated, irresponsible, frivolous, unreliable, wasteful, wild, indecisive, unresponsive, erratic, reckless, thrill-seeking, fear of freedom, a drinker, smoker, or over-sexed. Watch for these behaviors, thoughts or feelings and work to overcome them.

Wear the color turquoise or anything that makes you feel good. You will have a memorable day if you remain constructive and take advantage of the sense of excitement and adventure that's in the air.

## *6 Personal Day Vibration*

Today is your domestic day. Your sense of duty and responsibility are at their peak and this is the day to work them, because if any of the demands are neglected, they will rise up and strike you at a time when they would seem an impossible burden. In other words, don't start anything you can't finish today. If you start cleaning out your closet, finish cleaning it today. Same goes for doing laundry, wash, dry, and put it away. Keep your mind on the end result instead of on the mound of dirty dishes in the sink waiting to be washed. Try to keep busy and even-tempered.

This isn't a good day for long distance travel unless you're going to visit family. Close friends or family members may make unfair demands on you or be subject to emotional outbursts. Be understanding, and remember this is a day to show love and affection while taking on tasks for weaker or needier associates. Don't fall prey to martyrdom. Count to ten if that helps you keep your emotions in check.

Don't become a busybody or a meddler and wisely decide to wait until your advice is asked for. Be fair and honest with everyone. If you are in someone's bad books, or have argued with a loved one recently, then now is the time to bury the hatchet and say you're sorry. Don't force issues or go to sleep angry. Reconcile any and all conflicts today. Hug someone. It takes two to fight, and you might have to remind yourself that you may have had something to do with a misunderstanding or argument.

Today, the negative side of you might be prone to exhibiting the following traits: becoming anxious, melancholy, over-emotional, possessive, sacrificing, smothering, unkind, controlling, harsh, irresponsible, tactless, a perfectionist, unorganized, or resentful and regretful. Watch for these behaviors, thoughts or feelings and work to overcome them.

This is a great day for social gatherings, meetings, attending activities with your spouse or children, shopping for domestic purchases, or just visiting friends. Today, wear blue and concentrate on making others happy. Try to give out much in the way of friendship, love, and affection because the same or more will be returned.

## 7 Personal Day Vibration

Today, take your time, don't overextend yourself physically, and try to avoid confusion or conflicts. This is a time when you should be entirely alone for part of the day, to seek peace and quiet far away from people and distractions. If possible, go for a long walk in nature, spend a few hours in the country, or buy yourself some flowers. You need some time on your own to meditate, analyze, or just think things over.

Take a long look at personal plans, expectations, and your own character traits. Be honest with yourself and reflect on your past behavior to see how unproductive habits may be changed or eliminated. Visualize a healthier and happier you. Take care of dental or medical obligations.

Perfect everything you do, put on all the finishing touches, but don't try to make it larger or more productive. Don't take action or try to solve problems until tomorrow as solutions to technical questions or commercial delays will not be readily available. An expected letter or phone call may not materialize as others are likely to postpone making commitments or living up to their promises today.

If you keep still and wait, things will come to you, but if you go out after them you will be disappointed. Be patient. If possible, read informative books, go to a movie, listen to music, or just sit and think. Use your intuition. Allow your imagination to wander as abstract thoughts may turn into useful ideas or solutions.

Today, the negative side of you might be prone to exhibiting the following traits: aloof, antisocial, cynical, deceitful, devious, eccentric, fanatical, obsessed, hypercritical, immature, foolish, or having a lack of faith. Watch for these behaviors, thoughts or feelings and work to overcome them.

The key words for today are: Stop, look, and listen. Wear something purple. This is a good day for those of you involved in study or research.

## 8 Personal Day Vibration

This is your power day. Today, you possess a great deal of ability and power to make things happen the way you want. This is a day for big business and anything concerning finance or large-scale plans. All financial matters are favored as long as you know what your contracts say. Approach all matters in a businesslike manner; rely on yourself and express yourself with authority and self-confidence.

Feeble efforts, abusive language, and a fear of failure will only produce restrictions and frustrations. Taking chances and becoming angry or inconsiderate will not attract the respect this day has to offer. If situations become tense, be the one to maintain trust, dignity, tact, and responsible leadership.

Be particularly well dressed and appear successful. People in power are watching. Remember: Money attracts money. Today, you are likely to see debts paid or favors returned. Money may come in or go out for bargains, shopping, paying bills, promoting ideas, or socializing for business.

Your success is in your own hands. Focus on what you want and go after it. You will be successful as long as you operate constructively. You must also realize that money, material possessions, status and power are mere stepping-stones; success lies in the satisfaction that comes with material freedom and personal power.

Try to understand the needs of others and help yourself by helping those around you. Today's efforts may bring in the material rewards of tomorrow. Your success depends on common sense, logic and effective problem-solving.

Today, the negative side of you might be prone to exhibiting the following traits: abusing power, bullying, cold-blooded, crude, hot-headed, narrow-minded, rigid, scheming, unprincipled, disorderly, illogical, or lacking in confidence. Watch for these behaviors, thoughts or feelings and work to overcome them.

Wear something pink to help activate today's powerful vibrations. This will be a memorable day if you make a constructive effort to produce something tangible. Travel on business, but it's not a good day to start a vacation.

## 9 Personal Day Vibration

This is a particularly good day when you could achieve a great deal. Today is a wonderful day to spend with family or friends, for working with the disadvantaged, or to visit someone in the hospital.

Try to wake up with a pleasant word and be determined to settle all problems before the sun sets. Work involving a great deal of detail, such as ironing, sewing, filing, or talking to the accountant, may require an extra effort and should be put off for a few days, if possible. There will be odds and ends that must be taken care of and you may feel a strong urge to get everything out of the way. Use this day to tie up loose ends and expect nothing new to begin. Tomorrow starts a new cycle of achievement.

Today, try to be patient, indulgent, and full of good intentions. Don't stir things up. Take whatever comes in today, be agreeable, tolerant, and happy. Be prepared to make some sacrifices, take the blame for someone else's mistake, forgive and forget.

Today may also be a day of endings or completions. Endings tend to be connected to strong emotions and drama. Try to be compassionate, understanding, and sensitive to everyone no matter what the situation.

You should take stock of the possessions, occupations, habits, relationships, and pastimes that will never get you anywhere and eliminate them. Don't continue a relationship or experience you want ended just because your emotions are higher than expected.

Focus on culturally expansive people and meaningful experiences. Today, if possible, go listen to music, volunteer to give blood, visit an art gallery or museum, or see the ballet. Use your imagination, inspiration and intuition to express yourself artistically. Write, dance, star in a play, sing, or play a musical instrument. This is a good day for promoting yourself or for a public performance.

Today, the negative side of you might be prone to exhibiting the following traits: bitter, a defeatist attitude, unkind, unfeeling, unforgiving, self-pity, inflexible, intolerant, grasping, greedy, or victimized. Watch for these behaviors, thoughts or feelings and work to overcome them.

Although you'll be drawn to black colors today, it's better to wear colorful clothes to help brighten your mood. If pursued correctly, this will be a day of personal satisfaction coupled with fulfilled ambitions.

### 11/2 Personal Day Vibration
The 11/2-day has the same influences as the 2-day, except you will probably feel a lot of nervous tension. According to the way in which you handle today, you could either take a big step forward, or be thrown in another direction. You could be inspired by new visions of greater achievement, grow in understanding and sensitivity, or sink deeper into an old rut. It's up to you. Expect no personal rewards except through service and healing. This will be a day for thoughts and plans rather than for actions (read the 2 Personal Day Vibration next).

### 13/4 Personal Day Vibration
The 13/4-day has the same influences as the 4-day, except you will likely have strong feelings of limitation or restriction causing you to become rigid or lazy, looking for easier paths. You may become disorganized and find it difficult to apply yourself to the work at hand (read the 4 Personal Day Vibration next).

### 14/5 Personal Day Vibration
The 14/5-day has the same influences as the 5-day, except you will feel an excessive pull toward physical stimulation. You will be able to take advantage of this dynamic day if you change or curb tendencies toward restlessness, a fear of taking risks, or an excessive appetite for stimulation from food, drink, drugs, or sex (read the 5 Personal Day Vibration next).

### 16/7 Personal Day Vibration
The 16/7-day has the same influences as the 7-day, except today you may be on a different wavelength, have an argumentative attitude or be somewhat withdrawn. Family, friends, and associates may become confused by your moods, finding it

difficult to talk to you. Don't cause an argument with a loved one or close friend to gain time alone. Explain yourself clearly and let others know that today you need some time to yourself (read the 7 Personal Day Vibration next).

## 19/1 Personal Day Vibration

The 19/1-day has the same influences as the 1-day, except you might be somewhat self-centered, overly-aggressive, or indecisive. If so, don't use this day for significant beginnings because you may start off on the wrong foot. Realize that impatience, anger, stubbornness, selfishness, laziness, worry, anxiety, and arrogance will only cause you to lose control of situations that are in your hands. Change or overcome characteristics that could cause problems, then aim for the top and go after what you want (read the 1 Personal Day Vibration next).

## 22/4 Personal Day Vibration

The 22/4-day has the same influences as the 4-day. On one hand, this can be a day with vast power potential if you have pure humanitarian motives and little concern for personal gain. On the other hand, like the 4-day, it can be a rather dull, routine, and boring day. It's up to you to start working on important projects. Make big plans, but be realistic and sure you can accomplish your goals. You will likely feel a great deal of nervous tension (read the 4 Personal Day Vibration next).

# ABOUT THE AUTHOR

Debra Thiessen was born in Winnipeg and grew up on a grain farm near Springstein, Manitoba. She immigrated to Houston, Texas with her son and daughter in 1986. She currently lives with her children and granddaughter in beautiful Northern Idaho. She has studied numerology for over thirty years and uses it to help herself and others understand themselves a bit better.

www.ingramcontent.com/pod-product-compliance
Lightning Source LLC
Chambersburg PA
CBHW060936040426
42445CB00011B/882